T0123387

The
COURAGEOUS

OVERCOMING FROM WITHIN

CHRIS DEEROY

WESTBOW
PRESS®
A DIVISION OF THOMAS NELSON
& ZONDERVAN

WestBow Press books may be ordered through booksellers or by contacting:

WestBow Press
A Division of Thomas Nelson & Zondervan
1663 Liberty Drive
Bloomington, IN 47403
www.westbowpress.com
1 (866) 928-1240

Book page web address: http://dking1.com

Youtube channel for book movie trailer:
https://www.youtube.com/watch?v=sWhvA4Zt09g

ISBN: 978-1-5127-4586-3 (sc)
ISBN: 978-1-5127-4587-0 (hc)
ISBN: 978-1-5127-4585-6 (e)

Library of Congress Control Number: 2016909630

Print information available on the last page.

WestBow Press rev. date: 07/19/2016

CONTENTS

This is a true and uplifting story about the life of a young man at the crossroads of his life and his career. This book may help you answer some questions about your own life.

DEDICATION

I humbly dedicate this book to
The Lord Almighty
for showing me his infinite grace and mercy.
I also would like to thank him
for his blessings upon my life and
for all the loves with which he has blessed me,
for my lovely wife Happy, my children Davis and Brianna,
for my family close and afar,
for my friends, my extended family, all the wonderful
people, and even complete strangers who have at one
point knowingly or not helped me in my journey.
Thanking Sovereign Lord
for being with me every step of my life, and my struggles,
for helping me become a better person that I am
today, in his bright and magnificent light,
for being my stronghold in my darkest
hours, my moment of needs,
for forgiving my sins,
for answering me when I call onto him,
for opening my eyes, the eyes of my understanding,
for telling and showing me great and
unsearchable things I did not know,
for loving me and shining a much-needed
light on my path as I press forward,

for all the wonderful people he has brought into my life,
for supporting and guiding me in my journey,
and for his everlasting presence
in my life

THANK YOU

ACKNOWLEDGMENTS

Special thank you to everyone who has helped me at any junction of my life. I want you to know I am eternally grateful; I couldn't have done any of this without you. Thank you very much from the bottom of my heart, and may God bless you and your loved ones.

Special thanks to Betty and Joe Dolinsky for being my extended family, and for always being there for me. You will always have a special place in my heart. I love you always.

To Adjo Lemou and children, the Agbossoumonde brothers for being my other family. You are my brothers and friends for life, and have offered me a place to lay my head when I needed it the most. Your couches might not have been the most comfortable, but your brotherhood ran deep and will stay with me forever. Thank you.

To Geny Donohue of the On Point for College program. I don't know if you knew this, but you were a caring mother to me, and many others like me. You were and still are a true blessing from above. Thank you so very much for everything you have done for my brothers and I; I want you to know that we are eternally grateful. We will always love and appreciate you.

Special thanks to Messan for being my brother always. Thank you for inviting me to come to New York. Look where we are now! I know life hasn't always worked out the way we wanted it, but I want you to know I am thankful for what we have, our friendship and brotherhood. Love you bro.

To the Hart family, Melissa and Guy, and children: Mary, Missy, Guy and Christopher, for being there for us, my friends and family. We are forever grateful for and appreciative of you. Thanks and May God Bless.

Thanks to Frederick and Julie Peacock for also being our extended family. Julie, I will never forget that visit you paid me while I was still a college student living in my then tiny dorm room. I loved those snacks you brought me; they were delicious. And also sorry your shoes got stuck in the crevices of the paved ground. Thank you.

To Gwen Wheeler, thank you for your counsel and professional input. I am so thankful for all your help and for introducing me to Susan Doran. I also would like to extend my sincere gratitude to Susan for her patience putting up with me, and for fixing so many mistakes in my former project.

To Barbara Romeo, thank you very much for helping to edit and proofread my first project, the project I have temporarily put on hold for personal reasons. I am grateful for your honest and constructive feedback.

To Euan Viveash, you are my ultimate guide and a friend. Thank you very much for helping and for shedding a much-needed light on this project. I honestly believe you are God sent. Thank you very much and May God Bless.

To Akossiwa Chimene Agogo, who is currently attending University of Massachusetts Boston (UMASS BOSTON), thank you very much for your review and honest feedbacks on the project, and best of lucks on your upcoming school year.

To my brother Koffi, half a world away, and to everyone who has at one point kept me in their prayers; thank you for your prayers and May God Bless.

To the Ashenburg family, Robert (Bob), Alicia, Ben, Nick, Lauren, and Rene, I will always remember the dinners you fixed us after our soccer practices, and also for the occasional gifts under our Christmas tree. Special thanks to Bob for loaning me money toward my citizenship. I want you to know I have not forgotten. You come to mind every time I look at that certificate. Thank you.

To the Shoening family (coach Ken, wife, and children) for being one of the very first families to have welcomed us. Thank you for your help and continuous support. I want you to know we all love and appreciate you.

And last, but certainly not least: To Joyce Suslovic (Miss S.), AJ, and Brianna. Thank you for the countless rides you have given us to and from various places, at odd hours of the day, especially to and from school and soccer practices. Thank you for your patience in putting up with us. On behalf of all my brothers, thank you.

PREFACE

These are true and personal accounts of things. Some of these things you might even say are "astonishing" or "miraculous." I believe with all my heart that God has helped me in my life, as I am sure he has also done in the lives of countless other people, and maybe even yours. My hope in sharing my story is to help you or anyone in need of some hope and encouragement. If you are that particular someone, first of all, let me thank you for picking up this book.

I pray to God Almighty to bless you and help you, and that the book offers a personal answer to you and your problems. May he give you hope, strengthen you and your faith and be the guiding light in your life, as he has been in mine. May he who is Holy and everlasting help you in your journey, in your life in the name of our Lord and Savior, Jesus Christ.

Amen.

The Lord Almighty!

The Creator of Heaven and Earth and all there is in it. The one and only. The great "I AM." The God who once spoke live to mere mortal humans. He who created us in his own image for the sole purpose to worship him, still speaks today. To hear him is to hear his words. To hear his words, it helps to have a pre-disposed heart and the desire, the willingness to hear him who is Holy forever and ever. One must also learn how to discern his voice from the chaos that constitutes our daily lives. I personally wish I had known this sooner.

I came to know of God by accident; the same way many people are still searching and actually finding him today. Many of us usually call upon God only when we need something from him, which is good, because God actually wants us to call him in our moment of need. We are his children, after all; what else would he say? No? I don't think so. God still answers us according to our faith. God cannot be seen by you and me. In fact, the Bible states:

> "And he said, Thou canst not see my face: for there
> shall no man see me, and live."
> —Exodus 33:20 (King James Version)

If we must call upon an unseen God, would it not make sense that we first believe in him, that he exists and that he wants to hear from us and have a relationship with us?

This is where most of us often get confused, because we just don't know. We doubt the very existence of the God we call upon, yet expect our prayers to be answered. "Hey God, if you are there and can actually hear me; can you please give me this and that?" While some might rationalize that idea, I personally think it is a losing prayer, if it is a prayer at all. I also believe, God didn't think I was right about ever thinking there was such thing as a losing prayer. In fact, while God would prefer we know and trust him completely, he still hears and answers us anyway, in the midst of all our confusion.

I was once sick and needed to feel better. So I said some prayers not knowing if they would ever be answered. I was not even sure if anyone, let alone God was listening. That was me. I doubted deep down in my heart even before I made the first step, because that is the way many of us were brought up. We doubt, we second guess, we scrutinize, we underestimate, and we do not believe. We poke holes in theories and we question questions, because that is what we have learned at schools and in life. We learn in schools that things are not always what they seem. We were taught to think things through. This is why we sometimes overanalyze simple concepts and situations. We often have plan B(s) stacked up high to the ceiling, because we do not trust even our own good judgment at times. If so, how can we possibly expect to have our prayers answered when we have difficulties believing the very words coming out of our own mouths? But God still loves and answers us anyway.

I was in a dangerous situation once. I desperately needed help, and fast. In the heat of the moment, I uttered some words that must have been prayers. I cried for help like people often do, not knowing if my cries would ever be heard, let alone answered. I was fearful and uncertain about my future. I was in school, didn't have a job, and when I got out of school and still didn't have a job, I still cried out to God. With a mountain of doubts and debts piling up in my life, and my future looking so uncertain, I called for God. Was there a just God out there who could actually help me? We only call out to God when all else fails, and we can no longer carry on. Wouldn't it be better and more convenient to call out to him when we are not faced with any life threatening situation?

The intention of this book is not to teach you about God. This book is not even about showing you how to create, establish, or maintain a relationship with God; there is a Bible for that. The Bible is the word of God, and it has most if not all the answers.

This book is a personal account, a history of things, events and situations that have happened to me so far in this life. I believe, with all of my heart, that God has helped me through. It may serve as a miniscule reference point to help you navigate our ever confusing world. I am sure some of the things that have worked for me in my journey can definitely work for you in yours. And yes, God has communicated to me in some strange ways: sometimes in dreams, sometimes through pure intuition, and sometimes through deductive analyses. In doing so, he helped me make the best decisions pertaining to my unique circumstances. I am certain he can do the same for you, if he hasn't done so already. While you may not necessarily agree with me on some issues, God still speaks today. Just because you cannot hear his voice doesn't mean he doesn't hear yours.

I have come to learn that sins and immoralities have deepened greatly the astonishing gap that exists between ourselves and God. Together, sinful situations have kept us busy on things that do not matter to our well-being. They are the road blocks that have clouded our judgments, and in doing so have forced us to stop asking questions, forced us to stop seeking him who matters the most. This is because we humans were specially designed and made with the greatest care possible. According to the Holy Bible, we are the only species created in the image of the true and living God:

> "So God created man in his own image, in the image of God created he him; male and female created he them."
> —Genesis 1:27 (King James Version)

If we stop asking questions, then we will never find out the truth and miss out on the chance of getting to know God better. This is because we will naturally, and eventually, find whatever we are seeking, provided we don't give up.

God, in fact, clearly shows us in his ultimate manuscript, the Holy Bible, how to restore the original relationship he had with us in the very beginning. So yes, he also wanted us to really hear his voice so he can speak his words to us to help us during difficult times; to reveal things to us, and to lead us into his light. Also, it seemed God would not reveal himself to anyone who did not predispose himself, his heart to hear him.

If God did the opposite, he must have had ulterior motives that no one would easily comprehend, like in the case of the biblical apostle, Paul, who was then Saul. This is to say that God is able to see our heart, and even our innermost thoughts and feelings. In case you didn't already know the story, God – in the likeness of Jesus Christ – captured Saul, who later became Paul, while Saul was on his way to persecute, kill and imprison believers. This was not long after our Lord and Savior, Jesus Christ, was raised from among the dead three days after he was put to death by crucifixion. God's plan for Saul was to have him preach the good news, the gospel, to the very people Saul was persecuting. But how does that make any sense to anyone? This is a guy who was ready to go beat, stone, kill, and imprison any and all Christians he could find.

What did God do? He first stopped Saul because he could; he is the Almighty, after all. But not to kill him, punish him, or send him away to spare believers the agony they were certain to suffer in the hands of Saul. No! That was not why God stopped him. God stopped Saul to give him a second chance. God in his infinite wisdom evaluated Saul's heart and deemed him worthy of his grace; so he changed Saul's heart and gave it a 180-degree new direction in which Saul's life was heading, God sent him to preach the good news to the very same people he wanted to destroy. If this is not mind-boggling for reasons beyond comprehension, I don't know what is. But in God, anything is possible! The story does not end there. Please read the book of the Acts of the Apostles in the Bible to learn more.

INTRODUCTION

Most of us believe the lies we tell ourselves to justify the reasons why we cannot succeed and fail to accomplish great things in life, or why we find the journey exhausting and cannot find the strength to get back up when life hands us inevitable defeats along the way. Well, let me tell you something my grandmother used to tell me when I was just a few years old. She often looked me straight in the eyes and said, "You can do it; you can do anything if you want it bad enough." Then she slowly added, as if she could see confusion overwhelming my tiny body, "It is all in your head."

While it took me a great while to fully understand what my sweet old grandmother was trying to tell me; I finally comprehend her. She was just trying to tell me that I—essentially, my mental block—am the only obstacle preventing me from reaching my goals, and in order for me to break through, I first must let it go and actually convince myself that I too am good enough, strong enough, smart enough and qualified enough to do that which I aspire to do. Why am I telling you all this? Who am I and what actually qualifies me to tell you my story? For starters, I am somebody, a human being, and I think that is a good place to start.

I wasn't born with a golden, silver, or even bronze spoon in my mouth like some people would like to think. I have what most people would call a humble upbringing. Being born in a third-world country, in West Africa, and having survived my childhood despite my mother and father not wanting me when I was conceived. They thought they were too young to have a child of their own. They were in the process of aborting me when my grandmother caught up to my mother and saved, adopted, and raised me. Having also survived a political uproar and a refugee camp, and having to start my life all over in a different country away from everything I knew growing up, as well as my childhood friends, wasn't exactly something most people saw.

I grew up in Togo, where I saw poverty first-hand. And no, it was nothing like what you have in mind about poverty in America or in other developed countries. There was absolutely no welfare system, no health care system, and no government program of any kind to help needy families. I am talking about the type of scarcity that makes you appreciate and value life at its very basic level without regard to material possession because we didn't have much; that is to say, we didn't have any. We had to struggle for even the most basics of all: food, and a place to lay our head at the end of the day, every day.

In the year 1993, there was political unrest in Togo that saw many innocent people brutally killed; some people mysteriously disappeared, kidnapped and never heard from again. Those who were lucky enough to escape with their lives fled to the neighboring countries, where many perished, and some even before reaching their destinations. It was dreadful.

By the grace of God, some of us were granted asylum to the United States of America after seven agonizing years in a refugee camp, where another phase of our lives would unfold yet again.

I know poverty first-hand because I have lived it every day of my life, but I refused to use it as an excuse. I definitely didn't let it define me, as in giving me reason not to want to succeed. The opposite is true. I tried to channel everything I have learned along the way to help me reach my goals and where I am today, a happy place. Life was very hard. I was 16 years old and didn't speak the English language at all. I cried many nights just thinking about how to survive in this new and strange world, where everything was different from what I was accustomed to seeing and doing. Yet I didn't give up; I persevered. I worked hard, put myself through college, and most of all I believed in myself. I sincerely believed I too could make something out of myself, and that gave me a glimmer of hope. The fact that I had faith in God also made the journey that much more enjoyable, for I knew in the end everything was going to be just fine. He promised.

The following is something that has happened to me along the way, and I think God intended it for me to strengthen me, my faith, help me grow, and draw me even closer to him. My journey is not in any way too exceptional. In sharing my experience with you, I am simply hoping that it, my journey and what I have uncovered along the way, shed some light on your own life and journey, and hopefully guide you in your decision making as you move forward to bigger and greater things in life.

In all things, may God help you, and bless you abundantly. Amen.

CHAPTER 1

The Lone Warrior

We Are Never Alone, Even in Our Loneliest Moments

Man was God's finest creation. What became of him? Has he lost touch with his Creator and failed to have a relationship with his maker? If so, he would be but nothing: a lost soul and a desperate creature wandering the surface of the Earth. I once heard that man was God's greatest pride. He created him in his own image with the main purpose to make him proud, but also to rule over everything else God has created. Because of this noble task, man could be said to have a rather unique genetic composition.

He is born with certain distinguished characteristics that inevitably set him apart from any other living creature or thing. In fact, it is written in the Bible that God has called the mankind he created to be strong, courageous, brave, and unafraid but, most importantly, to listen to him, his Creator. While man was predisposed to have these undeniably wonderful and innate qualities and characteristics, listening to God or obeying him has been something man has struggled with the most. I know I did.

> But this is what I commanded them, saying, "Obey
> My voice, and I will be your God, and you will be
> My people; and you will walk in all the way which
> I command you, that it may be well with you."
> —Jeremiah 7:23 (King James Version)

In the past, God physically spoke to man, so I have heard and have read about in the Bible. I also believe that God, in his boundless wisdom, is still speaking today, but only to those very few who have learned to discern him and his voice. This is because listening to God needs some know-how. While we might never know what the exact requirements are to hear him from on high, paying attention to his ways, paying attention to his words, and trying to live a sinless life would be a good place to start. I thought I had once heard a clear message from God, heard his voice; my life has not since been the same.

The first time I distinctly heard the voice of God was in a dream. It was not so much of a voice I heard but a message I perceived. I had a very short dream that was full of meanings, and symbolisms that it took me a little while to understand. I had dreamed many times before, but this one was different.

It was a dream unlike any of my previous dreams. I felt in my heart that God was communicating a message of some sort to me. Although I did not clearly know what the intended message was in its entirety, right away, I knew it as a good message. I also knew it was meant to comfort me in my walk with he who directs my paths. A feeling of joy and peace came over me and made me feel reassured that everything was going to be all right. I knew then that I was going to be okay. This was something I desperately needed to hear, considering that I was going through a very difficult time in my life. Things were not going exactly well for me. I just had my first child, my son, and my professional career was on shaky ground. I was lost and confused about my future, and I had no idea what my tomorrow would bring.

In my dream, I saw a renowned star soccer player by the name Luis Suarez; I did not recognize him right away. Luis is a Uruguay-born professional soccer player who is widely regarded to be one of the best strikers in the world. He played for the English Premier League Liverpool Football Club during the 2013–2014 year and won the European Golden Boot award, enabling him to sign a multimillion-dollar contract with the great Barcelona soccer club. He became the third-most expensive player in the history of soccer. Luis was standing alongside a road with about 15 to 20 children, aged from 3 to maybe 13 years old. They were surrounding him. He must have just crossed the road with the children, it seemed to me.

This was at the back entrance road of the State University at Albany when coming from Western Avenue. I was actually running my usual route that day, a 3.2-mile trail simply known as Purple Path. Purple Path was one of my favorite routes; I had run it many times. That day I was wearing a long-sleeve, white, Liverpool Warriors T-shirt. As I was running I saw Luis, who was about 50 yards away from me, looking straight at me. He caught my eyes and with a big, broad smile on his face gave me a right-handed thumbs-up, which he held up high for a few good seconds as if to approve of me for something I was doing or to congratulate me for an accomplishment.

I saw Luis and his gesture, but I was too confused thinking about who he was and why he was giving me a thumbs-up to respond. So I kept running and thinking about it, until I completely lost sight of him and the children with whom he was standing. The first thing running through my mind was plain confusion. *Who is this familiar-looking guy, and why is he giving me a thumbs-up? Do I know him? If so from where?* I didn't recall. *Is he congratulating me, and if so, for what?* I had no idea.

As I kept moving forward, it suddenly occurred to me who he was. It was Luis Suarez of Liverpool FC, and of course I had seen him play on TV many times. I now felt terrible for not recognizing him sooner, and most importantly for not at least waving or gesturing back at him. Had I recognized him sooner, I might have even made a case for his autograph or done something memorable that I could share with my friends later.

Anyone living in Western civilization knew, or was at least *expected* to know, what a thumbs-up meant. Usually when someone gives you that, you are expected to return the favor. I could not help but feel bad for not doing so. A thumbs-up generally means good; it also implies that someone is happy about you. In short, it is used to pass a positive judgment.

Luis has been vilified for biting a couple of opponents on the pitch out of frustration, which has brought him suspensions and bad publicity. But Luis is also a great and heroic player who would do everything in his power to help his team win. He did that at the 2010 FIFA World Cup in South Africa, where he played an important role in his native country's fourth-place finish, scoring goals and blocking an extra-time goal-bound header with his hands during the quarterfinal against the Ghanaian international soccer team. For those who don't know the rules of soccer, unless you are a goalkeeper, intentionally touching the ball with hands is strictly forbidden during the game. Luis stopping the ball at the goal line with his hands was an act of desperation and a major violation.

Luis received an immediate ejection from the game, with the referee showing him the red card. That act saw him sent off the pitch while cementing his name in the hearts of his countrymen as a hero who saved his team from certain elimination. This was because Ghana failed to convert the penalty kick, which in turn enabled Uruguay to advance in the tournament. That day, both a hero and a villain were born in the same person.

What was such a person doing in my dream? That was the question I first asked myself. Maybe it was because Luis and I both shared a passion for the sport of soccer. I grow up dreaming of becoming a professional soccer player. That was a love I worked hard to realize, until it flew into thin air when I suffered a broken leg in a game.

While I still find time for friendly pickup games, I long ago lost my zeal to become a professional soccer player. Then it occurred to me that God was actually speaking my language. In this case, my love for the sport of soccer was the language being used to communicate with me. It was a realization that put me on the quest to know more. I wanted to know, right then and there, what the intended message was. I just *had* to know.

Why was Luis with a bunch of kids? That was something I did not understand at first. Maybe Luis liked helping children; he couldn't have fathered all those children, could he? I was forced to think deeper. *Could this be my guardian angel in Luis's appearance trying to get a message to me?* After all, Jesus was, if I am not mistaken, the only biblical character often depicted with a lot of children. He famously said to let all the children come to him because the Kingdom of God was for them and people like them. If that was true, then I must have seen a heavenly host. Luis could have been my guardian angel in disguise.

Why was I wearing the Liverpool long-sleeve T-shirt? The only valid explanation I concluded from the long-sleeve instead of the short-sleeve T-shirt was comfort, and to keep me warm. It was in the fall; the air was chilly, so the long-sleeve shirt made perfect sense. Luis was playing for Liverpool at the time, so seeing him in my dream while I was wearing his club's shirt could also symbolize my subconscious support or appreciation for Liverpool FC. Sport fans know more about this, and would most definitely understand my thought process.

With that in mind, it only made sense that Luis, a Liverpool warrior as all Liverpool soccer players were known and called, was probably giving me a thumbs-up, and so approving of me supporting his club. This could not be completely accurate because I wasn't then a Liverpool fan. While I like all the English Premier League teams, I am an Arsenal fan first and foremost. True soccer fans don't easily switch teams overnight; they don't generally support one team one day, and then move on to support another team another day. This could only happen in a dream. Could this, in fact, be God's own way of telling me to be strong like a Liverpool warrior, or simply a warrior for whatever situation I was going through?

On the T-shirt I was wearing was the Liverpool FC club's logo, in the middle of which was the mystical bird phoenix. As Greek mythology has it, a phoenix was a magical or mystical long-lived bird that was cyclically regenerated from ashes after dying in a fire. *What was the meaning of all of this? Could that somehow and all of the sudden have something to do with me?* As I continued to think, something clicked in me.

Growing up as a child, I didn't have anything to look forward to; my life was a constant struggle. To survive, I had to develop myself into a strong and resilient character, with a vivid desire to succeed. It was the only way. I just had to see things through without letting anything, not even failures, hold me down. Just like the phoenix bird, I too could not be shut down or killed so easily. While disappointments and setbacks happened along the way, I always found my way back up. Maybe that was what the power of the phoenix was all about, the spirit of resilience, and refusing to die, the spirit of life.

While I may never know what it all meant, going back through my thought process, I was able to isolate what I was able to decipher, and put them together piece by piece to help me uncover the tangible meaning behind the dream.

In recapitulation, I knew what the thumbs-up meant. I kind of understood what the children symbolized in this context. I was pretty sure what the long-sleeve white T-shirt stood for, and also the red bird within the logo. What it all meant together was something I was not able to grasp; so I kept looking.

This was also a time when I was feeling all alone and abandoned due to work-related issues; it was then easy for me to conclude that maybe God wanted to give me some sort of reassurance that he had not abandoned me, and that I was going to be just fine. I also thought that God must have somehow approved of me. I was convinced this could not have been a coincidence because I didn't believe in coincidence in the first place. I have always thought everything happens in life for a reason; not knowing the specific reason would not change the course of anything. It simply meant you did not know the reason. The word "coincidence" is just one of many terminologies people use when they don't know or understand why certain things are happening in the manner in which they are happening.

How could a simple few seconds' dream have literally given me so much hope and made me feel so much better, from the inside and out? *"I am not alone."* What a wonderful idea! In my effort to fully comprehend the symbolism behind my dream, I did what any normal, modern-day person with any notion of computers would do; I looked up the Liverpool Football Club on the Internet. You would not believe the first thing that came up during my search: a white T-shirt with the slogan "You Will Never Walk Alone" written in large, red print across the chest area. And the hairs on the back of my head raised. Wow! That must have been the bulk meaning of my dream: I would never walk, journey or in my particular case, run alone. That message turned out to be exactly what I needed to hear at that exact moment in my life. I was not alone!

As I continued to dig a little deeper, I have learned that the particular theme "You Will Never Walk Alone" was the title of a popular music hit from the past. The song was written by Richard Rodgers and Oscar Hammerstein in 1945. The Liverpool Football Club has since adopted the song and used it during their sporting events. It is the song Liverpool Football fans often sing to support their team during football matches. The melody became widely known as the Liverpool signature tune. And it went something like this:

Regardless of whatever difficult situation you are
going through, be strong, proud, and courageous
And don't let the darkness, or any dreadful condition frighten you
When everything is said and done, there is a reward awaiting you
At the break of the sun light, at the dawn of the day
Go courageously about your problems,
Go fearlessly about your life,
While people might laugh at your dreams and aspirations
Don't stop dreaming, don't stop dreaming
Be hopeful
And, you will never be forgotten, forsaken, or left on your own
You will never be forgotten, forsaken, or left on your own
Don't stop dreaming, don't stop dreaming
Be hopeful
And, you will never be forgotten, forsaken, or left on your own
You will never be forgotten, forsaken, or left on your own

I contemplated the magnificence of God as I carefully analyzed every word of the song. Tears came to my eyes, which I successfully managed to fight back. The funny thing was that Luis was not even my favorite player, but I have grown to appreciate him more now, as I have spent some time looking into why it was him and not any other person or player. According to Behindthename.com, a trusted online names directory, the name Luis is actually a Spanish, Portuguese, and Galician variant form of the Germanic given name "Hludowig" which means famous "warrior." I have always thought that I too have some of the qualities of a warrior. I am strong, determined, goal-oriented and resilient. What I love mostly about Luis as a soccer player is his pure determination and unmatchable zeal to win. Luis is a winner, and everyone can sense that about him. His presence in whatever team he is on is enough to send fear and confusion in the opposing team. Luis is able to break down strong defenses and score unbelievable winning goals because he is a fighter and a warrior.

While I might have appeared all alone out there, like I was in my dream: running alone down my usual path, away from everyday stresses, the anxieties and uncertainties of my future, I could now rest assured that I was not alone. What a wonderful realization that was! The assurance as that of a child at a playground, being supervised by the watchful eyes of a caring parent, suddenly came over me. We were poor. My grandfather, Whom I grew up calling Papa, was a retired machinist, who became a bicycle mechanic woke before the rest of us. While we all knew where he went, his under equipped small shop near a local church, we also knew he didn't make enough to support his family. Many nights, he went to bed hungry; so the rest of us didn't. This is because there just wasn't enough for everyone. That was the kind of man my Papa was. He always put his family before himself, and he would not eat unless everyone else had their fill. Those were the quietest nights of them all; and they taught me a great deal. I was not alone.

I felt at peace with myself, safe, and secured; I felt protected by an imaginary bubble, and I couldn't get hurt even if I wanted to. I could now be free and let loose and be myself again for at least a fraction of the time. I could worry less about my surroundings and my problems, and even my uncertain future, because I knew deep down in my heart that my God would not let me fail or get hurt. I have gained an unmatched level of confidence, so much so that my imagination was no longer what it once was. It had come to life. *"My footsteps! The noise of my footfalls as I was running; did you hear them? Can you hear them? Pauh.. pauh … - pauh.. pauh …"* If you listened carefully, between the noises of my feet, landing and taking off, my rhythmic breathing, the inhales and exhales of my still-beating heart were others noises. *Can you hear? "Pauh.., pauh.., - huhh.. huhh.. - pauh … pauh … - huhh … huhh …"* What you did not see was what you could not hear; those were the noises of my guardian angel hovering nearby, running with me, and making sure I was never alone on this trail, or any other.

CHAPTER 2

Hope and Courage

We Are All Unique, And That Is What Defines Us

Too often, we let our innocence or trust in people we thought we knew blind us from things we did not and would probably never know. These could be in some cases dark, dangerous or spiritual things that are meant to harm us.

However, not knowing, not being aware of an imminent dangerous situation or a hole in front of us would not alleviate any pain or harm it would have caused had we fallen into it. Our lack of foresight certainly and most definitely would not prevent us from the hurts, if we were to succumb and fall as result of our obliviousness. Ignorance, out of all things, should not be an excuse, or a viable justification as to why one did not take preventative measures. This was one of the reasons why I have learned to live with a pair of eyes in my mind. I had to, out of necessity, make a friend of vigilance, which meant keeping constant and watchful eyes for possible dangerous situations. It hasn't just become the norm; it has long become my second nature and my way of life.

As a young man growing up, I have learned a lot from observing. I have learned from other people's mistakes as well as my own. This was how I became acquainted with accountability, which is to me the art of taking full responsibility for my own actions, in both success and failure.

This has been proven to be a great and successful tool for my personal development and character building. However, keeping my eyes opened and paying close attention to my surroundings were, to me, valuable commodities—and this, against ignorance and needless excuses. If done right, staying vigilant can even be more valuable than gold and silver, because unlike gold and silver, being vigilant and paying attention can actually protect and save a life.

Anyone would be surprised by the number of warning signs a hypothetically unpredictable accident could actually have. More importantly, every important event, whether it is a natural disaster, a phenomenon, a man-made occurrence or anything hardly predictable worth noting always have forewarnings. To understand those warning signs is to pay careful and considerable attention to the loose variables before the proceeding event. Those variables could be as little as being able to detect a small change in the weather, the climate, a room, in the faces we see every day, the tone of voices of people we interact with, their facial expressions, and even unspoken body language.

All of these could communicate not only present events, but also that which are yet to come. Being able to compare that information and interpret its possible and relevant meanings, as they apply to distinctive instances, could literally mean the difference between success and failure, day and night, and even life and death. Humbling myself before the Lord Almighty and saying a prayer has always worked magic for me and could work for you as well. While all of this, and even learning to properly pray, may take some time and skills, the price of not doing it may sometime be too grave to pay. After all, ignorance, the feeling of helplessness, and not knowing something dangerous was to happen could be a very bad state in which one could possibly find him or herself.

I am a recent graduate from a prestigious university. I have carefully planned and thought out my career path and my future. I deeply and honestly believed I could have become anything or anyone I wanted to be, provided I sincerely and diligently apply myself. This was because I believed in my God-given talent and all the opportunities I thought were available to me at the time. This was my conviction. The expectations I had set before myself were sky-high. I refused to take any shortcut to my goals; to me those were red flags. I was going to take my time and apply myself the best way I could. With, of course, a few reasonable limitations, I knew I could reasonably accomplish some of the things I set out to do. I thought about bringing this to pass by being brutally and realistically honest with myself and acknowledging both my strengths and weaknesses. I knew I was as strong as my weakest flaw. So I focused as much time, energy, and effort needed to improve my weaknesses, as dismissing them could come back to haunt me.

In the end, I cannot be what I cannot be; I can only become who I can possibly become. No matter how great and exceptional my aspirations were, I had to learn to accept, to appreciate, to work with, and to respect that which I have no control over. I couldn't have chosen my birth parents, nor my siblings; they were given. But I could definitely choose who to be friends with and with whom to hang out.

The same way, I could move out of a toxic environment that was detrimental to my personal growth as long as I had the necessary means. While not everyone has the means to make certain changes, having the option is what is important. The truth of the matter is that one can only keep an eagle grounded for so long; sooner or later, it will eventually fly. The same is true for a lion cub and a butterfly, because they too are only transitioning through life, one stage at a time. The larvae will eventually turn into a butterfly and the lion cub into a grown lion, and so on.

What I couldn't afford to do was be irrational, like expecting a pig to fly. Logical thinking has helped me greatly find my way. *"What is reasonably within my reach?"* was my biggest question of the day. *"How can I realistically reach my goals?"* would have been my second biggest question. And, *"how can I do so without sacrificing too much of myself, or killing myself in the process?"* was another reality I couldn't forget to keep in mind. *"What could I afford to give up and still be able to have a fully fulfilling life? And what were my other options?"* Those were other important questions in the back of my head that I didn't need answered right away. Everything in life good and worth having always has a price tag. This I knew.

It costs to build anything successful; life just happened to fall into that category. That price, however, could be anything: time, energy, actual dollar figures or other resources. That was something on which we all could agree. In fact, that was the reason why I didn't need to have answers to all of my questions. But that wasn't the point. The point was, knowing those things kept me alive and in the moment.

I could have been a professional athlete, my dream and ideal profession, but things did not exactly work in my favor. A fractured leg in a friendly match during the summer of my sophomore year in high school put an end to that. I also could have been a visual artist, drawing and painting, which would have been the easiest thing I could possibly have chosen for profession. I had been known to be a decent artist since an early age and have managed to accumulate a list of prestigious art awards throughout my early years. Art was by far one of my most easily distinguishable and natural skills. For me, it was an escape. While this was good, I didn't see any challenge in doing the easiest thing that first came to me; so I decided to be thorough and comprehensive about my future. *What could have been enjoyable, rewarding and yet realistically challenging enough to enable me to reach my full potential?* I knew the answer to that question would translate to potential success even if success was for me - a simple concept. Being able to complete my education was to me a definition of success. Living a simple, peaceful and quiet life out of the spotlight would have been a success. Being able to come home every day to a peaceful and loving family that loves and believes in me would be my ultimate success. Success might be a relative term, but to me it is the littlest, often overlooked things that love is made of. While this might sound modest enough to you, for me it would have been a feat.

That is because most young people of my age group and from my underprivileged background did not have the luxury of a loving family, a peaceful home to go to, let alone someone to believe in them. They often go through life lacking fundamental support, the reason why many succumb one way or another to life's many obstacles. Knowing this ahead of time helped me plan my life wisely with no room for regret.

If I was to really succeed in life in the face of my adversities and my limitations, I needed to re-invent myself and be different. I needed to be supreme, or at least try to be supreme in everything I do. For starters, I couldn't take "no" for an answer and had to be my very best in everything I had the chance to do.

To do that, I required a guideline, a code of conduct, or a disciplinary mindset to hold me together. I became indoctrinated in the idea of having a mantra, a reminder, something to keep me in check and to remind me that this battle is worth the sleepless nights and the constant struggle to stay the course. In my struggle to find that balance, I wrote some random lines and pinned them to a wall where I was able to see them every day. It may not mean much, but as strange as it might sound, it helps visualize the journey.

Life is not a battle, but a dance, a platform
where battles do sometime happen
and where opportunities don't always happen
by chance; it is won through hard work
and a constant state of preparedness, and awareness
So I choose to be strong, wise and poised today, and every day,
for the road ahead is long, and unpredictable.
I have to be flexible and humble, on purpose for the greater good
To be smart yet ready to be let go at time, is not
a weakness; it is wisdom and a must
To be able to share a laugh with friends
and even a stranger is golden
I choose to be total and comprehensive in all
things, while living a life of no regret.
I must do everything I have the opportunity to do well
the first time for I may not get that chance again
To be fast yet willing to slow down just enough to have a
companion with whom to finish a race is an insight.
Why finish first, and run the risk of doing so in isolation?
So I choose to be fluent in life, for nothing is never what it seems
I must never stop learning, as in this is
the secret, and the key to success
To stay alive and relevant is to continue learning
To have a spirit of discernment, and be able to tell
the truth from the lies, is a skill worth pursuing
To always try to outsmart, and outperform myself in all things
Because I am unique, and created without equal;
I have to be my own fiercest competition
I must never accept defeat, only occasional setbacks
for God promised to never let me be defeated
And I will always come back from occasional setbacks
seven folds faster, stronger, smarter, and wiser.
I am good; I am enough, in God who created
me as I am, in his own image.

This was my reminder and code of conduct, by which I have tried to live by for as long and as far back as I can remember. While I didn't exactly remember those lines in that exact order, I did remember them. Together, they in part shaped me. However, trying to incorporate those principles into my everyday life wasn't always easy; it was a delicate dance between self-awareness and perseverance.

My coming into this world wasn't exactly a call for a celebration. Neither my father nor my mother wanted a child at that time. So no! I was not good news for either of them or anybody else for that matter. Neither side of my family was expecting my unannounced arrival. Story has it, families were joined together by faith, and I represented the connecting link. Unfortunately, I was a vivid reminder of mistakes they wished they did not make in the first place. Everything started when my maternal family rented an apartment from the paternal side of my family. This was after my mother's family consisting of my grandfather, whom we all called Papa, a strong-spirited and opinionated man, my grandmother Esther, my mother Jacqueline, her elder sister Elizabeth (Aunt Lisa), who later died not too long after my arrival, my uncle Jim, my late aunt Marie Sweet, and my aunt Tamar, the youngest of them all, moved in the area from a different city.

Had either side known what was awaiting them, or that they would be somehow linked for a long time, if not for the rest of their earthly life, they each would have forgone the opportunity to bring me into the world. My paternal grandmother Suzanne, the landlord, would have said, "Sorry, but I can't let you rent any of my apartments." And my maternal grandfather Papa would have responded, "Thank you for saving us all the trouble." But things didn't work that way. I was meant to come into the world regardless. It was very unfortunate; the conditions were not to anyone's liking. So I was conceived and birthed under a cloud of heavy smoke and judgments, as I was considered an accident child, a burden, and the object of all their predicaments.

While my timing was obviously the worst it could possibly have been, I had come anyway to stay, and there was very little anyone could do about it. I might have been minding my own baby business, but I also was, first and foremost, their collective business—sadly, the one they would have chosen to do without. Both sides of my family hated each other because of me; but I didn't mean any trouble. I came in peace, but it seemed they were not ready for peace, or me.

Rumor also has it that my late Aunty Lisa was the one who actually had the audacity to name me before passing away shortly after on suspicious causes. She named me "Hope and Courage." She felt the need to intercede and take precedence over my birth parents because neither of them wanted to take responsibility. They hated me enough, for I was the object of their shame and ridicule. It was also because of my paternal uncle Tito, who was plotting to get my father to name me an awful name per my mother's recollection, as one of his many attempts to get back at my maternal family. However, no one recalled that name. Tito was upset his younger brother had a child before him, and he hated him for that; it was custom that the eldest siblings got married and had children before the youngest. Names were then a prize possession and people didn't just name their children any name they wanted.

If a child was going to be answering to any particular name for the rest of his or her life, the least the parent could do was to take their time and give him or her a name that was thoughtful and meaningful. They believed the right name would set the proper course for the child's life and help determine who they would grow up to be. They also believed whatever name parents named their children—whether it is "success" or "failure," and there are names that reflect those things—that is what they would most likely grow up to emulate.

Naming was therefore a delicate affair. Aunt Lisa died shortly after giving birth herself to a son, her only son. Her husband

Timothy, who was a polygamous witch doctor, happened to have a lot of children, and as many as three-plus wives, with Aunt Lisa being the first wife. This was a guy who made his living from consulting dark spirits for people. What she was doing with him in the first place was a question to which we would never know an answer. Timothy, they said, had once saved me with his magic when my paternal family were determined to kill me, to put an end to the problem uniting my mother's family to them. Timothy, they said, brought my mother a juju necklace similar to a military dog tag without the identification tag with a strict instruction to tie it around my hip and never to remove it. He said: "it" referring to the enchanted necklace "will drop off on its own, and get lost when I am no longer subject of their," referring to my paternal family "evil attacks." This was in the aftermath of me getting really sick, and crying inconsolably at odds hours of the night. Timothy's necklace, they said, helped me through that period of my life; but what did I know? I was only a month old.

However, that didn't clear Timothy from suspicion regarding his involvement in his first wife's death. Local people, who have known the family for a long time, claimed Timothy sacrificed his first wife, Aunt Lisa, for his riches. And Timothy did acquire a lot of money shortly after Aunt Lisa passed away, though no one knew where he got it from. While there was no way to prove whether Aunt Lisa died from natural causes, or her own husband somehow killed her for money, one thing was certain: she named me. Aunt Lisa came up with "Hope and Courage" because she was hoping I would bring about hope for a better tomorrow, and the courage to endure whatever trial they were all going through at the time. My grandmother Esther once told me how Aunt Lisa wrote a special song, a lullaby for me, and she even sung to me the special song my aunt used to sing to me when I was a baby. It was a long forgotten nursery rhyme, about how Hope and Courage brought about peace and love into everyone's heart and the world. Peace was what Aunt Lisa had in mind, to mend everyone's broken heart.

Unfortunately, she didn't get the chance to witness her Hope and Courage sprung into reality; she didn't get to see me grow up to become the man I am today. May your soul rest in peace!

My mother called the police on her boyfriend, my father, and her mother-in-law, my paternal grandmother, for refusing to have anything to do with me and for refusing to pay my medical bills, which wasn't very smart. That sent the wrong signals and gave her in-laws a palpable reason to go after her. While my mother was logically justifiable, it wasn't exactly peaceful or the best way to get her in-laws' attention. It was nonetheless a mistake, probably the biggest mistake she, along with her entire family, would forever come to regret. But she got their attention: My paternal grandmother paid the 9,000 francs my mother had requested for the medical bills, an equivalent of about 20 U.S dollars.

Immediately after that amount was paid, my paternal grandmother had my mother and her family evicted from their property. She couldn't afford for them to use the unwanted baby to freeload off her; the property was her income, she said. That exchange was the catalyst event that started it all. With nowhere to go, and a month-old baby now under their care, my mother and family had no option but to leave. That was how I became homeless for the first time in my life.

Some friends felt sorry for my mother and family and helped them with a place, a temporary lodging until they found their own home. Needless to stay, the departure from my father's family house was anything but peaceful. There were lots of verbal exchanges from both sides; insults and curses were hurdled from my mother's side as they were from my father's side. Tito, my father's older brother, was the one who had to remove the door from the hinges to force them to leave before they were ready to do so. This was the ultimate insult and the utmost disrespect. My mother and family endured all of this because of me.

If Tito was right about my father, Christopher, spending seven years as a freshman undergraduate college student, this was nothing short of bewildering. How could it be? He meant it as an insult to his own brother, the only person to ever make it to college in the entire family at that time. Tito himself dropped out of high school; and although he has tried many times, he wasn't able to earn his high school diploma or its equivalent.

But, sure, they were then living in Togo, a country that didn't necessarily promote higher education and actually did very little to help its citizens excel academically. Even still, this was farfetched and downright unbelievable for someone like my father. Christopher might have been a father who was never there for me during my early years, but he was nevertheless a great student from what everyone knew. Those who knew my father during his school days personally referred to him as a genius, a bright mind, and an excellent student who was most likely to succeed in life.

If the story was indeed true, something must have happened to him; whatever it was, no one knew. My father finally obtained his Associate degree about three decades later in the United States of America, his country of refuge, and thousands of miles away from his birthplace, after a long break from education. That was also long after I completed my Bachelor's degree, making me, not him, the first person to ever graduate from college from either side of my family. That was nothing worth celebrating; nevertheless, I commended my father for his dedication and determination to finish that which he started.

Going back to my roots, I could actually name names of people, even close relatives and family members, who didn't know what success was. While success is a relative term, living and growing up around people who have seen failures and extreme poverty their entire life could alter one's definition of success. Furthermore, it could also make one feel immune to success; which was a dangerous place to be.

I have been in that place, and it was very damaging. I have seen people with my own eyes refusing the idea that success could one day also happen to them. They seemed to have lost all hope. That probably explained why growing up I was too serious in all things.

There were failures all around, with very little to no success story. They each predominantly dropped out of school at an early age because someone didn't help someone one way or another. Without the system of credits, credit cards, and student loans in place, tuitions or school fees were the main reason why most people didn't complete their education. Everywhere you looked, the stories were always the same. It always was someone else's fault, and never their own, even if the evidence was blatantly pointing the other way. Adding two and two together I already had a very good idea how my life would wind up if I was to do things the same way.

So I refused to play the blame game. I made the decision to not have any excuse, but to be true and honest to whom I was and about my choices. If I too was to fail, at least I knew I would have no one but myself to blame. Having an excuse, and having anyone to blame for my shortcomings, was against my belief system. While I might have been a product of my environment, I would not allow it to dictate which way my life went.

I believe I have the ultimate choice to veer my life in the right direction, the direction I so consciously choose. Hiding from my truth, which was my reality, would have been the end of me as an individual. As a result, I vowed to do things a little differently. This was how I have learned to own up to everything I am. While both successes and failures would eventually happen, it would be my approaches that would determine my outcomes. I have also chosen to accept mistakes of my doing as valuable learning tools, to help me grow and become a better me.

If I was to make a difference, any difference at all, I would have to own up to my own actions and stand tall. That was also why I have refused to celebrate small achievements. Passing an exam or getting a good grade at school, for instance, was ordinary to me; so why celebrate it? If I did my job right, like spending time preparing and studying for my good grade, celebrating would have been irrelevant. Good grades were by reason a byproduct of my efforts; I expected them. Bad grades, however, would have warranted a complete overhaul of my learning methodologies.

Thus far in my life, I have observed good and honest people often blindsided by small achievements, right before they were taken down and destroyed. Why risk extinguishing your inner zeal by celebrating too soon, a less meaningful achievement? I would rather save it for my ultimate finish line not yet defined. To celebrate, one would have figuratively raised both arms in the air like a boxer in a fighting ring, leaving the entire body exposed just for a fraction of time; a split-second window was all it took to lose any fight.

This is why life's small victories used to scare me. They were vivid reminders to always look over my shoulders, look behind my back, and check for any telltale sign of hidden dangers. Was I being distracted? Was I too comfortable? Was I feeling too secure? Was there a sudden change in the status quo, in the way things were always done? Was there a viable reason to support that change? Did that make sense? What were the specific contexts to which this and that applied? Was there something out of place, or did something new or unusual get introduced? Small achievements are good only when we don't let them get to our head. This is because they often are the best way to lose focus and to let the guards down and forget about the bigger picture.

For someone of my well-above-average intelligence level and overall technical background, I have always believed I would have a good career after college. While things didn't exactly turn out as planned, I didn't lose hope, because I knew everything would eventually work out for the best. My early not-so-flamboyant career path was a necessity to get me to where I am today. Before getting to where I am today, my happy place, I had to take a few unpredictable detours along the way. This is real life after all. Thank God those detours were not too scary; I am glad, for not having committed any irreversible mistake this far in my journey. I carefully weighed every single one of my steps, options, decisions and encounters, as I also did not believe in chance. Everything in life, whether good or bad, has a purpose and a reason; not knowing either behind any occurrence would not change its outcome. It certainly would not change the true meaning behind every minor or seemingly meaningless event that constituted life. Because everything in life mattered, the most seemingly useless and insignificant events, the ones everyone was quick to neglect, were often some of the most important ones. Together, they could hold clues to far more significant and greater events not yet known. So, I tried my very best to pay attention in life and not overlook minor important details, so I might not lose.

When I did catch myself losing focus, usually due to distraction, I always remembered to pray for God. I asked him who matters the most to please wake me up, to help me see what was hidden, to give me knowledge, understanding and the level of maturity required and needed to discern what really mattered in life and in all things. Yes, I have stumbled at a job or two. I voluntarily quit one or two, and I got laid off at one or two more. In fact, I was at a receiving end of the pink slip; when my first career job out of college company decided to lay off hundreds employees during the 2008 recession. Following that incident, I was forced to take a job at a wonderful local company that was too glad to book me for half of what I used to make for salary. A couple of years later, I had to let them go for a chance at rebuilding my career, and catch up with my quickly accumulating debt, even if they were some of the nicest people with whom anyone could work.

It was never easy, but I always tried to see the light in every situation and learn something positive out of an otherwise dark situation. Through it all, I never lost hope, because I had God on my side. It was at one of those not-quite-perfect jobs that I nearly fell victim to a co-worker by the name of Sally Voursheer, a blonde lady of about 50-plus years old. I secretly nicknamed her "the evil lady." In all fairness, I did not come to that denomination on my own. This was after I saw her in a couple of dreams in a form of a snake. Both times, the snake tried to bite me. This was a revelation that probably saved my life. This was because I was in a complete state of oblivion about what, or who, Sally really was. Those revelations jolted me wide awake and into a different reality I thought only existed in dreams.

What they said about never to judge a book by its cover was so true. Sally could probably have passed as one of the nicest and most helpful individuals you would ever meet. She was not; it was all a pretense. She was probably one of the very few people from the entire office who can confidently walk into anyone's cubicle, and start a small talk. Sally was a very eloquent, excessively friendly; and she could confidently make, even a complete stranger feel like an old friend. But, once you got to know Sally, she was a manipulative person with a dark cloud all around her. As I later discovered, Sally did not just like to help others; she loved doing it as a way to score points—points she could redeem for favors at a later time.

Sally made sure people gave her credit for helping them, and was more than happy to jump into job situations not directly involving her or her department. Sally must have owned the place, so it seemed. Maybe she did; after all, she was one of the very few seniors still working with the company. She was definitely not your ordinary sweet old lady, as she would have you believe. In my dreams, she was a sorcerer or something in that line who tried to kill me.

While Sally's role within the organization was a rather modest one, she seemed to always have her ways at connecting dots and people. She roamed free and did anything she wanted. So it seemed. This reminded me of something another colleague, Jeffrey Jamison, jokingly said to me at Sally's presence one of my very first few days of work with then my new company. He said: "I couldn't see you lasting long here at this company." That was after I had honestly answered what seemed like the most harmless and innocent question about the true meaning of my own name: "Dee." I thought that was odd.

At the time, Sally was in charge of training and bringing me up to speed, so we spent some time trying to get to know each other. Jeffrey, a close friend of Sally's, asked what it meant. Dee was a rather familiar and derived name in the maritime city of Lomé, Togo, where I grew up and spent a great deal of my childhood. For those of you who don't know, Togo is a small country on the western coast of Africa where I was born.

In the dialect of Mina or Ewe, which were primal dialects of the maritime city of Lomé, the name meant "courage" or "hope," depending on how it was used in a sentence. It is an action word. So I told them, my name stood for "hope" or "courage," depending on how it is used. I preferred both meanings, as in "Hope and Courage," like I did growing up even if courage is suggestively the stronger quality I associate myself with the most. This is because I don't sit around and wish for things to happen; I act, I do something, I take action. If used a certain way, my name means having hope or vividly expecting something. But if used another way by itself as a verb with a subject, it literally means "plant a heart," as in ordering someone, the subject, to "plant his or her heart." In the dialect of Mina, "planting a heart" means having courage or taking a strong stand and being firm in one's conviction. Jeffrey stopped for a moment as if to digest what I just said to him. Then he added another question: "Which of the two meanings would you prefer?"

In response to this, I quickly looked at him in the eyes, as if to see where he was going. Then I thought to myself, what difference would it make if I were to choose one meaning over the other anyway? As far as I was concerned, that was my name and I have grown to own it in its entirety. Then it occurred to me, he could actually be trying to make small talk, or maybe he was trying to assess me as a whole, starting with my most basic belief system, my mettle. Without realizing that they both were actually sizing me up, I decided to play along. "I love both meanings of my name," I replied, then paused momentarily to observe his reaction. Jeffrey didn't seem too eager about what I just said; he seemed to want more. So I quickly glanced around the office space, looked at Sally, who appeared amused by our little exchange, and flashed a semi-closed smile at Jeffrey without contributing a single word. While it took me a long time to realize what had happened, I could care less what their intentions were. I did really love the feeling my name conveyed, since they both were strong and powerful. Asking me to select one meaning of the two was almost heartbreaking to me. It was like asking a mother which of her twin babies was her favorite child. But a question was asked, and I felt compelled to answer, so I broke the silence and responded. "But if I had to choose one meaning out of the two, I would have to choose courage." At this, they both looked at me almost flabbergasted, not knowing I too was watching their reaction. That was when Jeffrey added his infamous remark, suggesting that my answer would have been the reason why I could not have a long tenure at the company. What happened there? Did I say something wrong?

According to the Merriam-Webster's dictionary, the online version, "Hope" was to cherish a desire with anticipation. Additionally, the word means to desire with expectation of obtainment, or to expect with confidence. It went on further to say that hope was the feeling of wanting something to happen and thinking that it could happen. It was a feeling that something good would happen. Courage, on the other hand, also according to the same source, was the ability to do something that you know is difficult or dangerous. It also said it was a mental or moral strength to venture, persevere and withstand danger, fear or difficulty.

However, to me personally, both words took on a whole new, deeply rooted belief system that transcended the conventional wisdom of what either word stood for. Hope and courage together, in some strange way, represented my being and who I was, am and would continue to be. I have been answering to that definition since my birth. Hope was to me an assurance and a promise. It was the assertion to see the end result of something, an event in mind from its very beginning. Knowing the end result of something at its beginning would make it almost impossible to go wrong. It was like having an immutable, unchangeable, deeply rooted expectation no matter how hard, or easy, or difficult or unsurmountable things unfolded in the beginning or the middle stage. Knowing the end result of something at its beginning was a game changer. This was also what I believed we have in God through Christ Jesus, our eternal hope.

To me, courage was having the audacity to firmly stand for what is right. This meant my rights as well as others'. Almost every battle in life is won through courage, and not necessarily through strength and wisdom alone. Courage is doing the right things in light of countless oppositions. It is fighting the urges to do what is wrong morally, physically and psychologically. It is accepting one's faith and putting on full armor and fighting the good fight of not giving in or giving up in the face of adversity. It is to refuse to stand by idly, and for taking the first steps to becoming a shining light and an example for all to follow. Courage is also about not taking the easy way out by doing just the bare minimum because no one was watching. For reasons far greater than ourselves that surpass basic human understanding, God out of all people called us to be not only strong, but also courageous. This was needed so we could be able to stand strong in the faith—to fight the good battle, to not give into corruptions, immorality and despairs.

So when I was faced with the question, I had a million flashes of light beaming through my mind at once. It was rather difficult and nearly impossible to split myself in two, to choose between "Hope" and Courage," because they belong together in complete harmony, in one piece, as I.

Subsequently, it is perfectly fitting to be courageous, while being hopeful. This we all can do.

CHAPTER 3

Behind the Veil

There Is Evil Amongst Us – What We Don't Know Can Hurt Us

W e live in a world where things are not always what they seem. Some people are not necessarily who they have others believe they are. What might appear to be an innocent question might very well have ulterior motives. Loaded questions, as they are often known, can sometime appear so harmless to the unsuspecting mind: But be wary, because they are not. They could be used to assess a situation or an individual, or to collect information that could be used for various different reasons.

Questions like the one my colleague Jeffrey Jamison asked me regarding which of the two meanings of my name, "Hope" or "Courage," I preferred wasn't just a naïve, random question. It was a calculated one, meant to evaluate me as both an individual and a potential target. My answer would then have provided a small window into my soul, my life by which to judge, and assumptions could then be made about me. Information collected could then be used to conclude or determine whether or not I was a threat. I wasn't, but they thought I could be due to my active prayer life. They wanted to know if I could be a member of their secret society, which I definitely did not want. Either way, they tried to evaluate my spirit—who I was and what my potential to them was.

I did not really know who or what Sally was at that time. And to be frank, I wasn't at all interested in knowing, or finding out either. If she and Jeffrey belonged to any secret organization, and they sounded like they did, I didn't know and I did not want to find out. And so reluctantly I answered Jeffrey's question regardless. I said: "I prefer Courage over Hope." As far as Jeffrey was concerned, that was my first mistake. But it was an answer, and it was my answer. He implied this could have been the reason why I wouldn't have a long tenure at the company. I neither knew nor understood what he was saying at that time, so I disregarded it.

What I thought was a joke three-and-a-half years ago and was long forgotten might not have been after all. It was a warning sign. Jeffrey certainly knew Sally under a different light than most people. And for him to say that my answer was wrong might not have been an accident, or an innocent remark, as I had thought. Jeffrey was talking from a different perspective, from a selfish first-person point of view and about things that only he, and a maybe a handful of other people, were aware about Sally.

I, on the other hand, could care less. I just wished we could work together in peace and without any animosity between us. This is how it was in the beginning as it was with the Earth. When I accepted the offer, it was good. But that was before I started to take notice of what Sally was actually doing. But once Sally noticed I was noticing her, everything changed.

What I began to realize over time was the fact that Sally somehow almost always found ways to get all the credit for other people's work, whether she was directly involved or not. How she did it was a complete mystery to me. It would also be true to say that I did not really care. There was very little I could have done to change her actions and manner. It also helped that Sally wasn't then sabotaging me or my work. Or if she was, I wasn't aware.

As a result, I went about my duties, and indeed the entire situation as I did with my life: selflessly and quietly, and keeping myself to myself. Nevertheless, I knew full well it was just a matter of time before she did to me as she had done to others.

As expected, Sally finally successfully pushed me under the bus, sabotaging and betraying me. This was thanks in part to a famous "John Doe" project that came across our desks. As always, I did not realize it at first; it took me some time to catch onto her slowly badmouthing me and taking credit for my work. What people didn't realize is that Sally was very smart in the way she approached her scheming. She knew if she was going to be effective at dominating the body, she first needed to master the head, and she did.

She had successfully wrapped Katrina Jones, our department manager, around her finger. I don't know what Sally did to Katrina to make this happen, but Katrina would inevitably always take Sally's side of any argument, issue, whether she was wrong or right. Knowing that ahead of time helped me a lot in identifying which battles I should fight and those which I should not. So what if no one gave me credit for my work? This was something I could neither fight nor compete against.

As a result, I left things alone and pretended I was unaware of her actions. After all, why bring forth the subject if nothing was going to be done? Silence then was golden. Why stir what could actually backfire? I was getting my paychecks when I should, and I had conscientiously decided not to lose any sleep over that which I had very little real control.

Subsequently, I behaved as if I were working for the Lord himself. For in the back of my mind, I knew in due time, he would certainly compensate me accordingly. As for Sally, I was not concerned at all. She was simply not my business.

The now infamous "John Doe" project was created by a particular client who thought that the company's strict rules did not apply to him. While that wasn't his first offense, we couldn't exactly hold that against him. It was because of people like him that we had a job in the first place. If anything, we should have been thanking him. The project was one of those cases no one really wanted to work. "John Doe" was a project destined and doomed to have undesirable consequences on anyone working on it. I just knew it. In fact, I spotted it a mile away. At the same time, I was obligated to work it because it was passed down to me from the approval department, where other colleagues had tried unsuccessfully to help the client. My job then was to fix the issues the best way I could, and moreover to get the financial numbers to tally so that the client could get funding for the project. There were deadlines to meet, so I went to work right away.

Those types of projects were usually burdensome, were time consuming, and required significant management approval, which always complicated things. Canceling the project model to create a new one however should have been the recommended approach. This would have been perfect if only the project didn't have a fast-approaching deadline. Consequently, that was not the correct approach for this case.

While our management team at the time were not the easiest people with whom to work, it did not look like I was going to be able to avoid having to deal with them any time soon, especially when I was fixing serious issues on project "John Doe." My work was sure to attract attention. Katrina had long failed to incorporate users' inputs into the design process of the new software systems. This predictably caused preventable issues to come back full circle and bite us in the back.

When that happened, management—the decision-making team—would go to great lengths in their effort to silence anyone who didn't agree with them. And they weren't afraid to do everything in their power to intimidate or even terminate employees in the process to send strong messages. Katrina has terminated colleagues with very little-to-no reason. This was in fact within her legal authority and was written in the employee handbook. In acting like this, Katrina and her management team had successfully managed to transform the workplace dynamic into a culture of fear and contempt and also caused a great divide among the staff.

Three invisible groups were subconsciously and mysteriously introduced: There were colleagues who blindly sided with management, those who did not but kept their mouths shut, and those who did not and chose to voice their opinions. Those siding with the management would do just about anything that was asked of them to show their loyalty and save their job, even if it meant sabotaging and betraying their friends and colleagues. They were secretly referred to as "untrustworthy." Those who disagreed with what management was doing but were too smart to voice their opinion because they cared—not necessarily about their job or the company, but mostly about preserving their only reliable source of income—they were the smart ones, and that was where you would find me.

Unfortunately, the third group was no more; they were no longer employed. They were the strong and brave ones, the sort of heroes who were not afraid to publicly judge and criticize Katrina or the management team. But they had dangerously overplayed their hands and suffered the ultimate consequence. They were either fired or given the option to voluntarily resign to help preserve their human dignity. That was how I lost two close friends and colleagues with whom I was hired and started working the same day. They were two very smart and talented individuals. What a grave and eye-opening loss that was to me.

In a culture of lies led by a "shoot first, ask question later" management mentality, everyone quickly learned to live in survival mode. No one would actually be naïve enough to say or do something as idiotic as giving one's honest opinion on a project, or anything else for that matter, without at least looking over his or her shoulders.

There were prompt retaliations for that sort of thing. The smart ones knew it and learned to practice self-control. They would carefully weigh their deeds, actions and honest views on things, however great, however innocent or however well-meaning the intentions were. Good deeds could actually spell disaster for individuals in those days. Something as little as an innocent, non-biased, good-hearted remark could spell bad news for the bearer or someone else. It was how simple fixes such as a claim processing, a task that literally took less than 15 minutes to complete, all of a sudden was taking longer than two days to complete, and not a soul could say anything about it.

More importantly, Katrina's management style miserably failed to incorporate one of the basic elements of a software development's lifecycle—that of bringing feedback into the design stages of the software systems.

Katrina's education and early career background might be to blame. She didn't have any technical background, and even her early career exposure was nowhere near technical. Whatever Katrina knew about management and technology she claimed she had thought of herself.

Driven by her ignorance on specific technical issues and her intense desire to succeed, Katrina chose to impose her iron will on her team. Why wouldn't she? She didn't really trust any of us. We all could easily see through her, and she knew it. That made her so very uncomfortable. So Katrina didn't know half of what she was doing, but she also wouldn't take "no" for an answer.

This explained why she was very impatient with her team, and even went as far as reverting some of the system access rights for the very people at the front line of her workforce. If the team could not access the production environment to assist the very clients we were hired to service, then what were we doing?

Katrina gradually turned into this fear-driven, and insecure person that everyone loved to avoid. To make matters worse, she had also knowingly declined to acknowledge and resolve preventable issues because she thought it would make her look weak. She was not afraid to silence anyone who did not agree with her. That was the reason why escalating a project such as "John Doe" would have certainly caused it to miss its deadline. So I went ahead and resolved the issues, but Sally Voursheer reviewed it, before pushing it forward through our systems.

Sure enough, the project was pushed back, but not for what you would have suspected. One of the approval managers decided to send it back because she didn't like the methodologies used to resolve the issue. A meeting was held behind my back with Sally in attendance. With Katrina on edge, Sally tried to distance herself from the project and I, in an attempt to protect herself. One good morning, Sally came to me, probably after a team meeting:

"Hi Dee do you remember that project? What is the name again …?" She pretended to have forgotten. "John Doe," she quickly added. "You worked on it a little while ago."

"Yes," I replied, "that name was not an easily forgettable name, especially after what I had to go through just to get the numbers to barely pass," I replied with a smile.

"Well," she replied, "it came back."

"Came back! That's odd," I replied with an exclamation. "What seems to be the problem?" I anxiously asked not actually realizing that Sally was trying to distance herself from the project and me.

"Well, one of the approval managers did not think it was modeled properly," she added.

"We already knew that it wasn't modeled properly," I added with a sarcastic giggle. "That was the reason why the client called us in the first place, wasn't it?"

"Well, they would have preferred you send it back to the client to be remodeled the right way; or you should have canceled that model and created a brand new one with the updated information before pushing the project through."

"You know too well we could not remodel a project that was pushed so far down the pipeline. It was already knee deep by the time it had gotten to us. In fact, the approval department sent it to me. If they thought it should have been dismantled and remodeled, they should have sent it back to the client, or said something," I replied, now in a serious-yet-polite voice, while always keeping eye contact with her.

I could already see the tension slowly building. I was actually reasoning with her instead of just saying, "yes madam" and blindly obeying. That was what she had been expecting. And that was exactly what I did not give her.

In the back of my head, I could actually see her exploding and burning with deep anger. Under normal circumstances, Sally would have explained to the approval management the basics of the project and the real reason why we needed to resolve issues the way we did before pushing the project forward. It was to beat the deadline. It was for the client's happy ending, and believe it or not ours as well. But she didn't, even though she was actually good at defending ideas. It appeared Sally was determined to let me take a fall for something that wasn't my fault.

"Well, sorry, but you made a mistake by not remodeling that project." Sally added harshly. "You now have to own up to it and move on."

Many things went through my mind, as I heard her address me in that tone. I could lose my temper, get in her face, and let her have a taste of her own medicine, but I didn't. I was too smart to fall for that trap.

"If I remember correctly," I patiently added, in a calm and controlled voice, looking her directly in the eyes, "I reviewed project John Doe with you in its entirety before pushing if forward. And you approved the changes, didn't you?" I politely proceeded, "I thought you approved my suggested solution and its implementation, and you even contributed a few pointers of your own. What has changed?" At this, Sally's facial expressions almost instantly changed. She went from hot burning to completely still and quiet. Without contributing a single additional word, she slowly dragged herself away and into her cubicle. I turned to my computer and resumed my work as if nothing had ever happened.

That was the last time we actually talked about the project John Doe. The truth of the matter was that it would have taken us more time to remedy at least a month's-old accumulated missteps, including a minimum of two weeks of absolute data collection and modeling. Our team already invested more than enough time in helping the client before the project reached me; remodeling it all over would have been a complete and total waste of time.

That project was a picture-perfect scenario, one of the reasons why the emergency guideline, which was a process specifically put in place to move problem projects such as this forward, was put in place in the beginning. Sally knew this, as did everyone else involved in the reviewing process. Yet they didn't do anything about it. The longer I thought about it, the easier it was to see that it wasn't about the project at all. Sally could have defended that project in just a couple statements and put an end to that issue. While I was not able to confirm whether she did it or not, I also knew she was too eager to hurt me to want to help me.

She was full of hatred, but that was her own problem, and maybe a little bit of mine as well. After all, I mostly like people would like to work in a hate free environment, if we can help it. Either way, I waited a couple of days to see what would happen. When I did not hear anything back from her, Katrina, or any approval manager, I logged into the system to investigate what had been done to the project since we last talked. To my eternal surprise, nothing! My changes were, in fact, the last documented changes to the project beside an approval stamp. That was it. So I thought to myself they finally came to their senses and moved on. No new talk, no meeting, no discussion, and nothing happened for a few weeks; and I thought it was over. Oh, was I wrong ...

What I did not realize was the fact that Sally was out to ruin me. She went out of her way to bad-mouth me to our manager, Katrina, whom she had successfully groomed for this type of occasion. After all, didn't Sally actually help Katrina find her footing on the job when she first started, and connected her to who was who within the company?

That must have warranted Sally special treatment and definitely a few favors in return; that was how Sally operated. She scored redeemable points. Gradually, the workplace atmosphere was beginning to deteriorate. And no one would ever suspect where it started from: the top, purposely orchestrated by none other than Sally, the evil lady.

Any smart person with heightened enough senses would have been able to smell the scent of degeneration in the room; something was just not right. And I could actually sense a predator closing in on me, trying to trap me and get me. I might not have known what my exact offences were, but I was pretty sure Sally had her hands in whatever they were. So, I decided to keep my eyes open and my ears attentive, and I tried my very best to stay on my toes and on my guard and not offend anyone. The last thing I wanted was to give anyone any reason to point their fingers at me. My ultimate aim was to preserve peace, avoid any possible conflict, and protect my good name.

It wasn't long before I had one of the strangest and scariest dreams of my entire life. In my dream, I saw a fat snake of a yellowish light-green color, completely immobile as if though dead. It laid immobile in my pathway as though waiting for a prey, or me. As I was cautiously approaching from the beach, leaving a large body of water, the Atlantic Ocean, behind me, something vividly told me to be careful, and that the snake was not dead. The beautiful, upscale, well-maintained, all-brick, two-story building house painted in pearl white color was my house. The snake stood between it and me.

I was wearing a flat sandal with the upper part of my feet entirely exposed and all my 10 toes visible. As I came close enough to the immovable snake, I stopped about 10 feet away from it and pretended to take an extra step forward, when all of a sudden the snake awoke and launched itself at my leading right foot full speed. I reactively jumped as far back as I was able. That was just enough to avoid being bitten. The fat snake had a very long reach for its size, and almost got me. It came about an inch away from my sandal even with me athletically taking a big leap backward. I was very lucky that time for underestimating the snake's ability due to its size. I wasn't expecting it to have that long of a reach. I quickly grabbed a good-sized wooden rod and chased the snake to kill it. But it somehow managed to escape. It had disappeared into a thick bush nearby. I had a very good look at the snake while it was launching at me, and I could swear even in my dream its face looked exactly like that of Sally, my coworker; it was as if she has morphed into that snake with intent to strike and kill me.

Still in my dream, I went to my white house. It had a nice gazebo at its open area. Still with the stick in my hand, I saw a lot of little snakes of multiple different colors crawling under the cemented floor of the gazebo. I immediately went to work, beating and killing them. I smashed and flattened so many of these small-yet-colorful little serpents, the entire place was beginning to look disgusting, stained with different splashed colors and snake blood and lifeless bodies. When I was done killing the little ones on the floor, I hit the leafy ceiling of the gazebo with my rod, shaking it and causing more snakes to drop down.

Again, I rained the beating down on them and killed them dead as I had done to hundreds of others. Then, in the corner of my eye, I caught the fat one that had tried to bite me earlier, slowly crawling up one of the gazebo's four cylindrical pillars. I immediately ran up, stretched my rod, and got ready to kill the fat and bigger snake, now that I had it in sight.

But as I was getting ready to deliver one of my most vicious blows, I distinctively heard my name: "Dee," I heard a familiar voice calling me. Who could that be? I quickly turned around to see who it was, and I couldn't believe my eyes; it was my mother. What was she doing there? "Mom?"

"Don't kill it," she said.

"Don't kill it? What do you mean don't kill it? This snake was setting an ambush for me; it was trying to bite me." Still covered in sweat as if drenched with water, I turned my head away from my mother, disregarding her request, and now determined more than ever to kill that snake. But it was too late. It has already crawled high up the pillar and into the bushy ceiling made of brown, dried, grassy, leafy material. I was frustrated and furious.

"I had it," I said to my mom, "I had it. Why did you stop me? Now look what you have done; it is gone." I was still furiously jumping and hitting the ceiling with my wooden rod hoping the fat one would fall down, but it did not. I quickly went about killing the remaining little colorful snakes on the floor, until they were all dead. As I was done killing them, I thought I heard my mother saying something to me in what sounded like a mocking chuckle. She said, and I distinctly heard her:

"You never know," she said, referring to the fat snake that got away. "It could actually spew me some money."

"What?" I immediately said in shock. I was more confused than ever. Since when did snakes vomit money? Why would my mother say something like that? She couldn't be working with them, could she? Why was my own mother there, distracting me at the exact time when I was about to kill the fat snake that mattered the most, the leader? Of course, she didn't seem concerned about my well-being, but that of the fat snake trying to bit me. All she cared about was how it could potentially make her rich. What was going on here?

I woke up from my sleep, still in a battle mood, fully alarmed and engaged. I was also heavily sweating, as if I just came back from a long run. It felt as if I had lived the dream; it felt so real, it was unbelievable. I quickly jumped out of the bed and turned on the light. Thank God, there were no snakes, dead or alive, around or in my bed.

I looked around, but couldn't find any. My breathing was heavy, and my arms felt tired, as though I had been delivering some blows, which I had been of course; but that had been in a dream. Or was it? Perplexed, but not afraid, I proceeded to the bathroom. After I urinated, I washed my face and brushed my teeth. On my return, I got down on my knees by the bedside to pray. I didn't know what that was, but whatever it was, I knew I could only beat it with prayers. That was a spiritual battle; and I would not even attempt to fight it on my own, so I called upon my rock, my redeemer, my stronghold, and my God.

Heavenly Lord, I call upon you tonight,
Because my enemies have conspired against
me; they tried to swallow me whole.
But I know, Oh Lord for your mercy endure forever.
Lord, I call upon you now for I have nowhere to go, and
no place to hide; but in You alone, I find my refuge.
Lord please deliver me, from the hands of my enemies
I call upon your Holy Ghost fire to come down from the
heaven and consume the snakes, wherever they are,
Burn, you snakes! Burn to ashes in the name of Jesus!
May every snake conspiring against me
be consumed by the Holy Ghost!
Father, I thank you for giving me this moment to come before you,
Thank you for your protection, for shielding
my family and I from the evil ones,
In Jesus Christ's name, I pray,
Amen

I said that short prayer before going back to bed, knowing full well that my God would not let me lose to these or any other snakes working against me. As I climbed into my bed, many ideas ran through my mind, but fright and despair were none of them. I did not try to make sense of the dream; I abandoned it all into God.

What that dream did for me was to revive and rekindled my relationship with my Creator. It reminded me how much I have neglected to earnestly pray. I was thankful for that opportunity. It didn't bother me if the fat snake was Sally in disguise, or if she was a sorcerer. I have worked alongside the lady for nearly three-and-a-half years, and have come to respect and appreciate her; I cannot bring myself to accept that about her. But if she was, I would have preferred that she not try to kill me.

CHAPTER 4

The Warning Signs

*There Are Always Signs Before a Storm –
Ignore Them at Your Own Peril*

The weight of contempt was in the air. It could not be seen, yet there it was. It could be felt. It was the weight of oppression pressing down on me, an employee of low rank, who was just scraping by, barely making a living. Someone in a position of power was bearing down adversely upon me, pushing me to the corner, slowly suffocating me. What had I done that was so horrendous and so unforgiving to be deserving of that kind of treatment, because I had not. I was a quiet, considerate and easygoing type of person. I did not go out looking for trouble, yet it seemed trouble had found me.

Nevertheless, my clear conscience did not stop me from tracing back my steps, digging for clues and answers in my attempt to figure out where I might have gone wrong. Both Katrina Jones, my department manager, and Sally Voursheer, my malevolent colleague, had been circling me like hungry sharks. All I could do was take precautionary measures to mitigate the situation I was dealt and pray that I didn't fall into any of their traps.

I also couldn't afford to fall victim to fright, despair or desolation; scaring me could be a part of their strategies. I needed to stay calm, collected and most of all, strong. I was determined not to project any sign of weakness, as I was sure it could only embolden them. Besides, I always knew I was going to be okay because I had God on my side. He promised to never let me be tempted beyond my strength and what I could handle. He would always work everything and every situation, good or bad, to my advantage. I believed in those words.

As a result, my heart did not shake, and my hands did not tremble. I was in a no-win situation where everything I said and did—my words, actions and efforts—were literally powerless and often used against me. It was a feeling I would not wish upon anybody, not even my worst enemy. Katrina Jones and Sally Voursheer conspired against me, and there was very little I could do about it.

My crime was being brave enough to voice my opinion and speak what I knew was the truth about a particular project. I was supposed to blindly agree to whatever they decided by simply saying, "yes," which I did not. That was my sole wrongdoing. The infamous John Doe project I thought I had long put behind me was the event that initiated it all. Unbeknownst to me, Sally had since used it to establish a case against me. I followed all proper procedures, but apparently that was not enough.

Because she had long wanted to put my head on the chopping block, Sally had seamlessly and clandestinely surveyed the entire office to find out whom I might ever have offended in the past. Sally was counting on strength of numbers to sink me. In her mind, the more negative reports she could successfully collect against me, the better her chances at building a strong case.

Out of the entire company of hundreds of employees, only one individual responded to Sally's silent survey. It was none other than her old friend, Cherise Sands, whom like Sally had been on the job for about the same time, nearly a decade. But unlike Sally,

Cherise had actually worked her way up to become an approval manager, which was about a fraction of an inch measuring stick above the pay grade of both Sally and me.

That was also a title Cherise embraced with ultimate pride and a hint of arrogance. Never ever have I met anyone who was so proud of her job title. She was a project approval manager, and she was going to make sure you knew it. Cherise reviewed projects other people worked hard to create, reviewing and comparing numbers against the government-mandated approval numbers and criteria. If the numbers were within the specified range, the projects were approved and pushed forward. If the number were below the range by a certain margin, projects were ejected with a comment and pushed backward for someone like myself to resolve.

This was where Cherise, or any approval manager for that matter, was needed. Just like the janitor who diligently cared for the bathroom, or the secretary who politely answered the phones, Cherise's job was equally very important. An approved project meant business, and a potential financial value for everyone involved. A failed project meant the exact opposite, and no one wanted that. A failed project was a waste of time and resources that could have been put to a different use; plus, no party would get paid.

Cherise, on the other hand, was notorious for making her analysts' lives miserable by giving them unrealistic timelines and expectations for random assignments. Why? No one knew for certain, but it seemed Cherise enjoyed doing just that. Maybe that was who she was; she reveled in others' unhappiness. Cherise was notorious for putting those below her even lower in order to make herself seem higher than she actually was. That was what she did to her team ever since she became an approval manager, and she got away with it because no one said anything.

She had run over her subordinates over the simplest mistake and harshly criticized them, some to tears. Cherise was the loud type who was always right and would never admit she was wrong; even when she blatantly knew she was. What I didn't know was that she too hated me. There had been an email exchange about six months ago. In that email, I had unintentionally given her a reason to hate me. I dared offer her my opinion in an open forum on which many colleagues responded.

"The best way to help clients from committing preventable errors such as the ones you were referring to," I wrote in an email, "is by educating them the first time around. We can do this by first letting them know the first time we come across the errors, and then show them the right way to do it. In doing so, we will not only be mitigating our workloads but also hold clients to a certain level of accountability. Not to mention that this will save time and help the client hopefully get it right next time."

I responded to her email in which she stated there was nothing we could do to help clients make certain mistakes. That marked the end of that email communication. Cherise neither responded nor talked to me about it. She secretly despised me for offering what I thought was my honest opinion in an open email. In her mind, I should have let her make me, and my department, look bad because she and her team waited too long before informing the client of potential errors in the design. This was in a wake of her team blindly trying to force a project through with known preventable mistakes. And, I wasn't even trying to correct her.

I could understand Cherise being upset at me for not agreeing with her, but what I did not understand was why she was holding a grudge against me for something so pitiful? Now it seemed I had unintentionally silenced her; a grave offense punishable by a severe reprimand explaining why she has joined in on Sally's crusade in her attempt to punish me. Cherise did what any vengeful person would do: She printed the email, highlighted key words in my response she was certain were offensive and handed it over to Sally. Sally, in turn, did the same with some past emails we had exchanged and handed them over to Katrina without my knowledge. Just like that, the case against me started.

Katrina was insecure and very sensitive and often had very little to no time trying to figure things out on her own. As a result, she tried to rely on scare tactics by bringing down severe judgments for minor infractions. While we might have not agreed with Katrina's decision most of the time, we were smart enough not to voice our honest opinions; those were dangerous propositions. When I started noticing Katrina acting funny in my presence and trying to be rude to me, I immediately knew something was up. Something must have been said to her behind my back, causing me to fall from her good side. And that worried me a lot because I have always been very careful dealing with her, because I knew the type of person she was. Otherwise a nice and wonderful person, Katrina seemed to have allowed too much power to get over her head; but she probably wouldn't be able to tell. Maybe it was the combination of long and stressful work days, the lack of proper family life balance considering she just became mother again for the second time not too long ago; couple that with Katrina's habit of quickly jumping to conclusion without completely analyzing issues or situations. While Katrina processed many wonderful qualities, it was probably her volatile personality, and her desire to be liked by everyone that may be hurting her image. And I would never have said nor done anything to contradict or upset her.

That was not a good place to be. Katrina was, in my opinion, a manager who should not have been a manager, because for one, she was too emotional. But who was I to judge? It was no news that everyone in our Information System Team (IST) knew Katrina did not have the "it" element necessary to lead a group of that caliber. In the same token, everyone admired her tenacity and efforts play-acting her way through every situation. For her, it was an art.

It was an art that enabled her to get the job done, thanks again to her team and her unorthodox ways of approaching technical issues. Katrina managed to maintain a pristine image with the upper management by building a personal relationship with them. It was a confusing relationship none below her dared question; it was also a relationship that saw her promoted to the head of our IST department over people more qualified than her. And no one said anything.

Katrina had figured out that hiring outside consultants and implementing out-of-the box, pre-designed software packages, instead of enabling her team to apply their technical expertise, would seal her from open criticisms. That, however, wasn't enough to fill her other voids, such as her lack of both technical and managerial skills. She didn't care; she would fire anyone who didn't like or agree with her. Katrina graduated from college with a four-year degree, majoring in biology. She had previously served as an assistant high school biology teacher job and somehow found herself managing a group of computer scientists and software engineers. While she was not capable of coding a single programming language whatsoever, she got to tell computer scientists and software engineers alike with many years of experience perfecting their crafts, with degrees from reputable and prestigious college institutions, how to do their job.

Katrina was power hungry and filled with paranoia. But, she wasn't always like this; in the beginning Katrina was considerate, and understanding. Something changed; and I certainly didn't know what it was. Now not agreeing with her on any issue was to become her enemy. Becoming Katrina's enemy was to be booted from the company, provided she could find your replacement in a timely manner. While no viable reason was in fact needed to terminate anyone's employment at the time, finding suitable replacement personnel was not necessarily easy. That was what prevented her from dismissing some people she didn't like, at will. It also forced her to grow up and learn to work with people who didn't always agree with her. Either way, I didn't want to be Katrina's enemy. It would have left me with only the following two options: One, I would have to start looking for an opening elsewhere—that was, if I wanted to advance my career—and two, I could actually try to work my way back to Katrina's good side. This was a lot harder to do because she was avoiding me and wouldn't talk to me. The third and final option was hoping and praying that over time, the situation would self-remedy. The latest approach was the most dangerous of them all, because people didn't just change overnight.

So I decided to give option number two a try. But after a few unsuccessful attempts to schedule a meeting with Katrina bore no fruit, considering she had canceled our bi-monthly, company-required, one-on-one meetings indefinitely, I thought all hope probably was lost. I had observed Katrina, on more than a few occasions, trying to avoid me altogether. Things were beyond repair. When I personally caught Katrina on multiple occasions stopping by Sally's cubicle, which was adjacent to mine, greeting everyone in her path while passing before my cubicle without any sign of acknowledgement or greeting, I was greatly amazed. Hard to believe, I actually really liked her. I thought she was a nice person.

I could not have believed my own two eyes. How do you meet and talk with someone who does not want to see you in the first place, let alone talk to you? It was just a matter of time before she acted on it. If I had one last wish before parting company with that workplace, it would have been to let Katrina hear my side of the story. Knowing full well that she might not be interested, at all, it would have brought proper closure to both of us. Chasing after her could have been a risky proposition. I would patiently wait for the right moment to talk to her, even if that moment never came.

That was how I went about my daily activities without much regard for what anyone said or did in the office. Whenever the opportunity enabled me to interact with anybody, I either politely declined or made it very brief. I asked very few questions during team meetings and briefings. I tried to get my work done in isolation and limited my overall involvement in the office life without looking like an outsider. I was just being careful, with my eyes wide open, while I patiently waited for the opportunity to explain myself. More importantly, I waited for a sign from God about what to do next. I prayed.

I had long learned, at an early year age, to submit to God my plans and intentions, and he would bless them and bring them to successful fruition in due time. What happened when I did not even know what my plans or intentions were was something completely different. To get away from it all, I tuned myself into an audio Bible at my work station, thanks to an online Bible channel and a headset. It was a gateway unlike any other. I even went on leaving the headset in my ears without any audio output, just to signal to others not to disrupt me when I was working. It was during one of those moments that I overheard something that was not intended for me to hear. Katrina walked over to Sally's cubicle to get her point of view on a project she needed help understanding. They both chatted for a while, when Katrina stated: "Dee has been awfully quiet these few days. I wondered if he has heard anything."

"I don't think so. He has been tuned into his music a lot these days, minding his own business," Sally added with a smirk.

"I hate this kid. I want to kill him," Katrina added to my amazement, as if she and I had been in some kind of quarrel. To this, they both giggled. My cubicle was just one step away for Sally's, and we could clearly overhear each other's conversations all day long. There was basically no privacy. Why would she say something like that in front of me? Was she joking? Then it dawned on me. She hated me so much that she was avoiding me. In fact, I had overheard that conversation only because they thought I was tuned to some music on my headset. That message wasn't intended for my ears at all, and I was glad I knew how they felt about me.

While I was disappointed, I wasn't angry. However, knowing that information could only help me to know how to deal with them both. That meant I needed to start looking for another job right away, and hopefully find one as soon as possible. It also meant that I was warned; possible provocations and even assaults might be in the future, something I sincerely wished I'd never have to face. At that moment, talking to Katrina was the last thing on my mind, even though it could help shed some light on my side of the story. Whether or not she would give me the benefit of the doubt was outside my realm of control. For now, I needed to stay alive, and that meant being vigilant, and mostly respecting the distance she had put between us, herself and I. Just a couple days after that incident, something else happened after I left work. David Cooper, another coworker who had the habit of being the last person to leave the office, came in the next morning with what sounded like a spooky story.

"Hey guys!" exclaimed David right before our regular standup morning briefing, "You would not believe what happened here yesterday about 15 minutes after everyone left the office." A daily standup briefing was a brief team meeting where individual team members were required to update the team on what they were working on, and if there was any issue or impediment that may present a road block for any task going on at the time.

"What happened?" replied Thomas Sinclair (Tom), another coworker who seemed vividly anxious to know.

"There were some spooky noises from that part of the cubicles," responded David, now pointing at where both my cubicle and Sally's were located.

"Oh really," replied Tom.

"Yes, strange scratchy noises, and I couldn't tell what was making them." David paused a minute to read the faces as he was sure no one would believe him. Then he continued. "I don't know; they were scary, high-frequency, harsh, irritating noises that sounded as if someone was dragging something pointy on a metal surface. I first thought it was the cleaning crew, so I called: 'Was anyone there?' To which no one responded, because there was no one there. That was when I quickly booted my computer, put it in the bag and left the place in a hurry." He completed with laughter. "You know me. I wasn't in on any of ghostly stuff; I was out in a flash." To that, everyone laughed louder— everyone except me. But David couldn't stop there, so he continued. "That noise, there was something about it. It sounded more like something or someone was dragging something, like tools."

"Farm tools, maybe?" quickly added Sally. "There could not be any farm nearby, right?" she added amusingly, trying to diffuse the tension.

"Maybe, it was, I had no idea. I was out of there before whatever it was started farming, or whatever."

To that sound, everyone laughed some more. While my mind was racing trying to connect some sort of dots, I was actually happy I was not around to actually witness whatever David was describing.

Katrina, who dialed into the morning briefing from a remote location, added, "That is weird and spooky, don't you all think?"

"Oh, this reminds me of something I had seen from the parking lot the other day," added Tom. "If I am not mistaken, I have seen a flock of ravens, a lot of them, flying up and down, and probably mating atop the roof. Ravens are known for making crazy noises. Could that be it?"

"I don't know what it was, and honestly I did not stick around long enough to find out," responded David with a smile. "The minute I heard those funny noises, that was it. I was out. I wanted nothing to do with that."

"Hahaha," laughed almost everyone, except me, who remained seated and quiet, still trying to make sense of the new development.

Just a few days ago, Katrina was telling Sally how much she hated and wanted to kill me; and now crows started to pay us a visit, assuming crows were making those noises?

What I knew about crows and ravens came from movies, books and the Internet. I knew they are smart birds: dark and spiritually unclean. I had also learned that they are very social animals, and the only one out of a whole list of birds to pass judgments on their own kinds. And they never fly in isolation; when you see one crow somewhere, the second crow must not be too far behind, observing. I also knew that crows don't just suddenly and randomly show up at someone's place of residence, or in this instance, a place of employment, by accident. Something of sinister significance must be behind their presence. Crows were commonly associated with bad omens, as they were believed to be cleaners of decay and messengers of death. In some of the movies I watched a while ago, sorcerers and witches employed crows as their third eyes. In one other movie, they were sent to announce an imminent death waiting to happen. They were bad news, and so their sudden presence at my workplace was definitely not a coincidence.

"Well, as long as they were just doing that, I think it is ok," said Katrina, referring to the crows on top of the roof. To this, everyone started to get up because it was the end of the briefing. Right at that very moment, as if by appointment, we all heard some funny noises coming from above my cubicle. Sure enough, there were a bunch of ravens flying, landing and moving right above us. We could all see them because my cubicle was located exactly under a skylight, which was a transparent roofing material in the ceiling, specially designed to let in sunlight, and so brightening the room.

"Come see guys," David said quickly. "I think they are back again."

My cubicle was momentarily transformed into a showroom, except the show was happening on top of the room. But since the sun roofing material was offering everyone the front seat of the house, why even bother going outside or climbing on top of the roof to see it?

"Wow, this is dangerous," I thought to myself. "This is very dangerous," I silently repeated back to myself while everyone else was laughing, trying to imagine what kind of mating ritual was going on right on top of our heads. I knew the crows' presence was a tell-tale signs of something sinister just waiting to happen. If what they said about the birds held any truth, they were there to remove the dead or the dying. The question was, who was the dead or the dying in the place? Not me; if Katrina had Sally mark me for death, they were dead wrong. Armed with that information, I knew right then and there I was in for an all-out war.

I knew with actual certainty that one and two things were spiritually happening: One, someone had commissioned an evil spirit to carry out some mission at that workplace. And two, whatever was going on was purely spiritual and dangerous. Adding two and two together, I quickly realized that my life could be in danger here, for I could have been marked. While there was no sure way for me to determine this, I would rather be wrong and take some preventative measures than be right and not do anything about it.

As a result, I patiently waited until everyone moved to their respective cubicle, and then I said a short prayer before sitting down. Even this bothered me tremendously; so I got up and went to the bathroom, because my heart would not possibly accept the thought of a bunch of dark birds doing their ritual right on top of my head without me doing anything about it. If I had my way, I would have gone on top of the roof with a big laser gun and blasted all those birds dead. But I did not have my way, and I did not own a laser gun. So I did what I knew how to do best: I prayed. I went and locked myself in the bathroom to pray. I called upon my God, my refuge and my stronghold. I did, and he answered me!

Father Lord, I come before you because, you are
my God, my stronghold, and my savior
You alone know the situation in which I find myself.
You know how my enemies have outnumbered me
They are fast closing in on me, and seek my downfall
They are preying on my weakness and my
innocence, and want to erase me

from the face of the Earth.
I have nowhere to go but to you.
I pray to you oh Lord to please have mercy on me
Please show me your kindness and redeem me
oh Lord. Deliver me from my enemies
Lord please do not let my enemy boast in my down fall.
Please don't let them ever say where is his God?
Where is the God in whom he so trusts?
Lord show them that you alone are God, and you alone can save
In the name of Jesus Christ, I call upon Holy
Ghost fire to burn those birds to ashes,
Be consumed, you dark birds, by the fire of Holy Ghost!
There is no relationship between you and
me; I belong to the Light, to God,
In Jesus Christ's name – Amen

I didn't need 15 minutes to pray that prayer, but I needed some time alone with my God. While the bathroom might not be the most ideal place to call on God, I was sure he didn't mind because he had answered me. By the time I got back to my desk, there was not even a squeak of a bird of any kind to be heard on top of the roof or nearby. It seemed as though a scarecrow has gone on top of the roof, or were they consumed by the Holy Ghost fire?

I wasn't surprised they were gone; I was thankful to God for intervening in my favor. I believed I was not like everyone else; why would I? I was redeemed by Christ. Unlike most people, I, along with most believers, did not respond to calamity the same way. We do not panic and run around in despair. This was because we actually have a hope for being washed clean of our iniquities by the blood of Jesus Christ, for being forgiven of our sins, and for being redeemed; because of this, death has no dominion over our life.

Because we do not belong to ourselves, and our Lord and savior has overcome death, we now have the assurance of true freedom. Provided, we believe in what is already ours, and claimed it. Unless we do this, we could be free yet still live in a state of bondage, which is worse. Later at home, I called on my family and briefly explained to them what I thought was happening. They agreed to help me in prayer; so we prayed together as a family. I also brought the issue forth to my local Church, dropped in a prayer request on the issue, went forward and had Pastor Jeremy Goods pray for me.

I also talked to a couple of our church elders, who were equally glad to support me in prayer. I had both the support and the arsenal needed to win whatever war was waged against me. I thought I knew what was required of me to be acceptable to God, and to receive his infinite mercy; I just needed to go to him as I was, and he would take care of the rest. Knowing God was eternally holy, I also decided to sanctify myself and seek his face. With the help of my family, in a common accord, we decided on three days fasting. In those three days, I principally saw myself transformed, for I was able to see the love of God, and his mighty presence in my life. It was one thing to be told God loved you, but to feel it and experience it was something entirely miraculous. At the end of the fast, moved by the Holy Spirit, I opened up to him.

Oh Heavenly Lord, my Lord and Savior
I thank you for this moment you have given us to
come before your throne, and seek your presence.
We seek your Face for this battle is not
ours to fight, but yours all alone.
Our enemies meant to harm, but all it did,
was bring us even closer to you.
I am deeply sorry for leaving you out of my life all these years.
I am deeply sorry for wanting to do it all on my own.
Now, I pray, help me Oh Lord, for we want to stay close to you.
We want to be near you, we want to be in your Light.
Please give us the strength to do so.

Before you, everything is Possible,
Before you, all mountains lay low, our enemies
flee, and our problems evaporate
Lord Oh my God Thank you! Your mercy endures forever
You have given us power and authority to ask in
your Holy name and it shall be given to us
Whatever we bound on Earth shall be bound in Heaven and
Whatever we bound in Heaven shall be bound on Earth.
In the name of Jesus Christ, I set on fire
every evil spirit standing against
Your will for my life and that of my family
I burn them all to ashes wherever they are,
and wherever they come from,
May it be the depth of the deepest ocean
The heart of the earth, or even from the sky above
I set them all on fire in the Holy name of Jesus!
Burn to ashes!!! – You crows, you ravens, you evil
spirit, messenger and servants of the evil ones
Burn to ashes you evil spirits wherever you are, for
there is no relationship between you and me
Because me and my family we belong to the Lord
In the name of Jesus Christ—Amen!

Those few days before, the Lord rekindled my prayer life and certainly made me feel a lot closer to my Creator. My heart was open, and I felt an overwhelming joy and gladness reverberating from within me. I was beginning to feel lighter, and lighter on my feet. I elevated my heart and my cause to the Lord, and I was sure he was going to handle business. The next day after the fast I went to work as usual. The only thing different this time around was that I now began to pray and commit the day and everything in God's hand before I sat down. A week had passed since the birds visited us at work, and I was even beginning to forget about the entire incident when Sally, who rarely spoke to me after our little project John Doe discussion, suddenly stopped me on my way to the cafeteria.

"Hey Dee" she said "What happened to our birds?"

"Our birds? What birds?" For a moment I did not know what she was talking about because I had almost forgotten about it. Then, it became clear to me that she was referencing the flock of crows that came to the roof of the office, not too long ago. I became almost speechless, and I knew exactly what happened to the birds. They were burned and toasted. That was what I asked God in my prayers, to burn them. So no, I wasn't surprised they were burned to ashes.

But why would she, out of everybody, ask me about the birds if she did not know anything about them? Sally must have had something to do with those evil birds' sudden appearance. Did she send them, or did she have someone else send them? I almost exclaimed and asked her one of the questions above, but I caught myself and refrained myself from doing something atypical or uncharacteristic of me. I quickly regained my composure and answered her in one of the most neutral, yet peaceful, voices you can imagine:

"Oh, those birds, they were burned!" I honestly and confidently said as if I knew firsthand what had happened to them; then I continued on my way to the cafeteria. My answer took Sally by storm; she literally froze and became momentarily speechless. The look on her face gave her away; she did it. Sally's face quickly changed expression from curious-inquisitive to ghostly dead. She really looked as if she had seen a ghost. I would never forget her mesmerizing stare as she slowly dragged herself back to her cubicle.

Wow ... I kept thinking to myself, *this stuff is for real. Oh wow! With whom am I dealing here?* I had a thousand light bulbs flashing through my mind simultaneously. My heart, on the other hand, was beyond rejoicing; it was singing songs of praise to my God and my savior. I was surprised, and at the same time happy, about what I was sure God revealed to me. I could not wait to go home and tell everybody, especially those with whom I cried out to God. At home later that day, I broke the news to my entire family; together we offered our thanks and praises to the Lord, who showed me and my family his mercy.

Something must have really happened behind the curtain because Katrina, my manager who hated me to the point of wanting to kill me; who had been avoiding me for a few weeks now, suddenly wanted to meet with me. She sent me an Outlook invitation to discuss some projects, my learning objectives, my personal time off (PTO), and the upcoming company picnic. I had all kinds of red flags going off in my mind. If that was not a miracle, it must have been a trap. Katrina really hated me, wanted to kill me, had been avoiding me, and out of nowhere wanted to meet with me? This could only mean one of two things: One, it was a miracle; God had softened her heart to hear me. Or two, she found out about the hand of God on me, how he had saved me from their death trap; as a result, she wanted to be nice to me, so I didn't torch her with my prayers like I did those evil birds. I had already agreed to meet her, but I also knew I should not go in expecting a miracle. She could be trying to fish information out of me, information she could later use against me. That much I knew, and I was going to be careful.

The company's annual picnic was almost upon us, but unlike in the past, this time around I had no desire to attend. I could live without the burgers, the nachos, the chips, the sodas and the beers most colleagues were not even allowed to enjoy responsibly in the upper management's presence. Those people where hypocrites in the sense that they would have everyone believe it was OK to let loose; but if the meeting somehow went just a little out of the line, or someone drank more than one or two beers, they were the first to judge that same person. I wasn't going to have it; I wasn't going to be drinking—that is, if I ended up going at all. While I have attended the same picnic the past three years and actually enjoyed it, this year was different. I had never looked over my shoulders at any job before in my entire life like I had been doing at this company in the past few months.

It was not fun. Besides, I also did not want to go because both Katrina and Sally might be using that moment as an open platform to get back at me. They could poison my foods or drink if I wasn't careful enough, or they could possibly ridicule me in front of the company's executive management. Thanks, but no thanks. I went over many different scenarios in my head just to avoid going to that picnic. Telling Katrina that I did not want to attend it would have absolutely given her a new set of ammunition to use against me. She would have loved to tell everyone; starting with her management team, how horrible of an employee I was. That was something I was sure she had probably already done. Plus, I would not have wanted to stay in the office all by myself while everyone else was out picnicking. I could also have called in sick, but that would have made me a liar. It too was not something I wanted to do. I discussed the issue with my brother Emanuel, who advised me to go. He also reminded me to pray before I went. That was something he didn't need to tell me. I was already on my guard. He knew me well enough to know it was redundant to tell me to pray, but he did it anyway.

For some reason, Katrina wanted to meet with me before Friday afternoon of the company picnic, which was less than a week away. I was able to tell she was up to something because she personally and awkwardly came to my cubicle earlier in the day to remind me. There must be some connection between the upcoming company picnic and the meeting. It was unusual of her to come in my cubicle. This only heightened my suspicion of her. Sure enough, the meeting was but a moment away, and I would soon hopefully find out what she had up her sleeves. Who knew? I too might even have a chance to explain myself regarding the project John Doe, and maybe Cherise's email.

For the day I had on a khaki pant with a light blue, short-sleeve dress shirt and topped it off with reading glasses. The glasses gave me the allure of a sharp business man. The picnic was right after work, since we were supposed to work a half day, but I did not want to dress down. Most of my colleagues wore shorts and T-shirts for the day; not I. I felt the need to be at least presentable, yet not too overdressed for the occasion. There was not much going on in the office that morning, so I spent my time answering just a few calls and responding to a couple of old issues. It did not take long before Katrina sent me an email to come to her office. I said a little prayer before joining her in her office.

Katrina had the nicest office space on the entire second floor, overlooking the large parking lot. It was not the only one, but definitely one of the very few offices with windows to the outside. The rest of us were living in a cube farm, with no access to windows. While Katrina's office was not the biggest, it was spacious enough to house two of our regular cubicles. In it, she had an executive desk separating the room in two. In the back end of the room was her executive chair and what looked like a very relaxing and therapeutic beanbag loveseat.

Katrina had a couple of pictures of her couple years' old daughter and of her husband directly facing the door as if to say, "Hey look, here are my greatest loves." Expectedly enough, the visitor chair was not as comfortable as the executive one she was sitting on; but it served its purpose. It was not meant for anyone to be sitting on it for a long period of time. It did not recline and looked as uncomfortable as it felt. Behind her, was a small bookshelf with less than half a dozen books nicely distributed with the book titles facing the entrance door as if to say, "Hey look, here are the books I have been reading;" which was odd for someone even as insecure as she was.

"Hey Dee, come on in," said Katrina the minute I entered the door. She had been expecting me. "Please have a seat," she continued, pointing at the visitor chair directly facing her.

"Thank you," I answered. "I really appreciate you taking the time out of your busy schedule to meet with me."

"Oh, don't mention it," she said with a chuckle. "I have been meaning to do this for a while now, and sorry it didn't happen sooner. I have been very busy lately. But I am glad we can now catch up. How are you?" she comfortably added with a smile, as if she thought she could actually charm me.

Knowing too well what she was trying to do, I replied in the same tonality of voice she engaged me, matching smile for smile.

"I am good, thank you." I then waited a few long seconds before filling in the silent void. "How about you?"

"Good," Katrina quickly replied, and continued as if she did not like me asking about her well-being. Maybe she wasn't doing well, and my asking her about it only reminded her how she was not really doing so well. I thought to myself, "This is getting interesting already!"

"Where to begin …? There has been a new development at the company headquarters explaining why I have not been in my office lately. This also explains why I have not been very religious with the team meetings and the personal one on one. I don't know if you know, but I have been promoted to the company-wide general IST manager role, which means we now need to hire my replacement to help with our local stuff." Without giving me any time to comment, she continued, "I have seen on the company learning and development site that you are on your way to meeting your yearly goals this year, which is good." Goals were some arbitrary employee development tools which basically helped upper management decide whom to promote or not to promote. It was neither an accurate representation nor a reflection of someone's actual performance or competency. It was rather a simple indicator of an employee's willingness to grow, which the company was hoping would translate into productivity. Katrina being promoted to a general manager position came as a total and utter surprise to me and the entire team because, as I and many from her own group could attest, we didn't think she was even qualified for the local manager opening in the first place. I first thought it was a joke, but it was not for me to say anything about that; so I kept my mouth shut.

"Anything about the goals you want to discuss today?" Katrina added.

"No, I think I am good in that area," I responded, because there was really nothing to discuss there. I was on track from the beginning of the year. I carefully selected items I knew I either had already completed or I would not require any assistance completing. Looking back, I was glad I went about things that way. It would have been degrading, awkward and even suicidal to ask someone you knew hated you for help.

"PTOs," continued Katrina, "I saw that you requested a few days off. Would you mind elaborating on that?"

"Yes, I did, and I am glad you brought that up. I needed both the Friday and Monday after Thanksgiving off. I will be traveling to see friends and family." To be honest, I lied about that. In a way, I felt constrained to lie, or Katrina would be shutting me down right then and there. Sally also requested that Friday off, and we both couldn't have the same day off. In fact, Sally had been getting that day off every single year since I started working at the company nearly three and a half years ago. So I was determined this year to do something about it. I too would be out either shopping or enjoying time with family like everyone else. It was time I made a stand, and I did.

"Well, I don't know if I am going to be able to give you both the same day off. That is because Sally …" I knew exactly what she was about to say: because Sally also requested the same days off. So I politely stopped her.

"Sorry to interrupt you, but Sally has been getting the same Friday after Thanksgiving off for the past three years, while I stayed here and worked. Don't you think, maybe, it is only fair I too get this one off?"

"I think you have a point there," she said, now raising her head to look me in the eyes. "If Sally had the habit of requesting and getting that popular day off, then it would only be fair that you too get this turn." Katrina paused for a moment, as if to think about the consequence of what she just said.

"Please remember to put that on the team calendar so I can approve it."

"I already did," I answered, still maintaining eye contact with her. It was company policy that managers approved PTO before the employees went on personal leave. The funny thing this time around was that she knew I already placed the request on the team calendar before talking to me, yet she felt the need to ask me to do it again. That was something I did not understand right away; but it later made sense. Katrina was afraid of Sally because she had promised her the same Friday after Thanksgiving off, so pretending she did not see my request in the calendar would have been a perfect excuse not to grant me that same day. Doing so would have allowed her to approve Sally's, if she hadn't already.

"Anything else you want to talk about?" Katrina asked while pretending to be taking a note.

"Yes, in fact there is," I responded, and waited for her to look at me before I proceeded. When she did, I said, "You must have heard of a certain John Doe project, I am sure."

"Yes, I remembered something John Doe-related coming across my table," she responded. "Is there something else I need to know about it?" she added directly, looking into my eyes. Thank God I was wearing my glasses that day, for I felt it added a little bit of a barrier between her and me and gave me a bit more confidence.

"That project was a mess from the very beginning." I said to her confidently. "The client used an unorthodox approach to modeling the project while trying to make the numbers pass, which was understandable, but still wrong," I quickly stated from an expert point of view. "I just want you to understand that by the time the project reached my desk, an unsurmountable amount of energies and resources had already gone into it from both the client's end, as well as our from internal staff, who have unsuccessfully tried to help." I continued, "I could have disregarded everything and remodeled the project, pushing it back a couple of weeks, but I didn't. This is because that would not have been the best approach given the circumstance." I stopped to make sure I didn't lose her. When I realized I hadn't, I continued: "I wish you realized I am currently the best at project modeling using our software systems." This was no news: the entire office knew about it; project modeling was one of my many specialties.

"Yes, I know you are, but we were trying to get every client to adopt the best methodology when it comes to processing projects from end to end. I only wish you had informed the client of that fact before processing the project for him the way you did and moved it forward."

"I did" I assuredly replied. "I certainly informed the client of that fact, and also about the correct way to model the project." I continued, "Not only that, I also worked with him remotely, showing him the best alternative way of working that type of project. I went above and beyond to make sure that the project met the deadline."

"Oh, never mind the approval department," Katrina stated. "I am not sure they really know what they are doing down there anyway." Then she said something I did not expect her to say. "I thought you did a great job handling that situation."

"Thank you." What I did not understand was, if the project went through successfully after I manipulated some functions and algorithms to get the number to pass, then why did no one even bother to tell me? And why was Sally trying to make me accept blame where there was none?

"Is there something else you want to talk about?"

"No, thank you," I responded.

"Thank you, and see you at the picnic," she concluded.

I then got up and exited Katrina's office, feeling about 10 times better than I had going in. All of the sudden, I did not feel so nervous about going to the picnic. I even thought about changing into a soccer jersey that had been collecting dust in the back of my car trunk.

CHAPTER 5

The Picnic

God Works in Mysterious Ways

It was time for the company picnic again. The venue last year was a local well-known public park. The scheduled time for the event was one o'clock. But since most people never show up at a party exactly on time anyway, let alone at a picnic, I decided to take my sweet time. I deliberately wanted to arrive late. I had also decided on not picking up any passenger to or from the venue. Providing transportation to the venue was to promise myself an early arrival.

Arriving there early would most likely get me assigned some type of responsibility. Whether it was a cooking job, fixing the tables, adding some finishing touches to the setting, or worse, being forced to socialize with upper management staff where saying the wrong thing could end up following me or anyone long after the party and might even cost more than one was willing to pay, were all things I didn't want.

After driving around for some time, I finally arrived at the picnic about 45 minutes late. Good! By that time most people who had been invited were already present and ready to have good time. On the other hand, I was indifferent. I was no longer interested in the event. I only wanted to show my face because I had to: Katrina's order. I too, much like my colleagues who did not want to be there, had to endure the moment. More importantly, I hoped not to do or be involved in anything that would cause me to stand out in any possible way.

I planned on being invisible and unnoticed the entire time. I wanted everyone there to feel as if I was not even there. Knowing Katrina, as an emotionally unbalanced person, who desperately felt the need to impose her will and wants on others, and who had ties with upper management and just about any influential person at the venue, it was safe for me to stay low-key. For all I knew, she might have already made me the bad guy in some of their eyes. Staying invisible might have given me the benefit of the doubt, and maybe make everyone who might have heard her say how terrible of a person I was second guess her.

The picnic took place in a local public park, under the same pavilion we were given the very first time I attended exactly three years ago. I vividly remembered everything: the place, the setting and every little detail as clear as if it were yesterday. The park sits on a spacious 130 acre-land, situated just a couple miles away from a small airport behind it, and about a mile away from a large shopping center before it. And, it's wonderfully designed to accommodate many recreational activities, needs, events, and even formal events such as weddings.

On the right hand side of the two one-way streets leading traffic, and people into the park, was a large three-acre pond with at least three sprinkling water fountains in it. You wouldn't see anyone fishing or ice skating in it, like the sign said you could. But, a dozen or so beautiful migratory wild geese with a couple of their goslings could be spotted swimming at any given time. Between the pond, and the large children's playground equipped with three straight slides, a circular slide, a big play house with many games, and about five swings, was the first main attraction: the splendidly designed club house, which was equipped with a circular gazebo with what looked like an observatory all-glass upper-level. There also was a fabulously designed deck overlooking the pond where visitors could, if they so wish, feed the wild geese, or fish without ever getting their feet wet. There in the club house, formal events usually take place. The second main attraction was the new addition, the all-inclusive fitness center in the far right hand side, in the back of the park, and on the edge of the three miles running trail it overlooks. The park also includes many different types of trees, meadows, marshy, wetlands, a small maze made entirely of trees, wooded and wildflower areas.

While our pavilion was one of many there, it also was the farthest, in the far left-end of the park, from the main park entrance. It stood about 12 to 15 foot high in the air, with a vaulted ceiling held together by eight strong pillars, two at each corner. There was absolutely nothing unappealing about the park.

It was raining that day, as it did every year. Upon my arrival, I quickly found a seat at the edge of a long bench and quietly sat down with my eyes plunged into my cell phone. I did not want to be bothered. The food was mostly already cooked. They were neither great nor bad; they were tolerable. Barbecued chicken breasts, drumsticks and hot dogs were on the menu. There also were some green beans, lettuce, tomato, soda, cookies, potato chips, homemade apple pies, crackers and some drinks. Also on the menu for the day were some trivia games and other fun activities for everyone to partake in, with prizes associated. While everything else seemed to have remained exactly and predictably the same, there were a couple of unusual additions to the prizes people could win. Unlike three years ago, this year we could actually win a dinner with the company vice President. While this might have been a great idea, it didn't interest me. This is because I was trying to maintain a very low profile, and that meant avoiding people, and staying out of most pictures. The second and final new addition was an organic new microfiber blanket with the company name embroidered on it, which I thought was a good idea.

Seated somewhere in the middle of the pavilion on a wooden bench, I was surrounded by people from different departments, all trying to carry some sort of conversation. It turned out to be a blessing in disguise, as I used that opportunity to quickly learn the names of unfamiliar colleagues. I felt people were looking at me; the last thing I wanted to do was to call someone by the wrong name.

That would not have been good. Unlike what some people would like to think, I am not perfect, I too have flaws. For starters, I was terrible at remembering people's name. This always has found ways to come back to hurt me. Calling any sensitive person by the wrong name at the venue, could have given that person a reason to paint me in a negative light; something I didn't need. Besides, if I was to be quiet and nearly invisible, I had to avoid introducing myself like some of my colleagues. I ended up dodging and avoiding many people by pretending to be helping, sometimes at the grill, and then pretending to be taking frequent calls, or doing something seemingly important on my mobile phone.

After we all ate and drank, the company vice president, Mister Duck Mushier, took the podium. Everybody welcomed him with a big round of applause. He then went on to say a few introductory words and proceeded to greet everyone for bracing the weather and coming to the picnic. Was it coincidental that every single one of the company picnics in the past three years ended with rain? I didn't know, didn't understand, and probably never would. Mister Duck Mushier personally and briefly made a reference to that, because the weather had been nice earlier.

He then thanked a handful of people, congratulating them by name for jobs well done, before congratulating the entire team for a very successful year. It appeared the company recorded near-record profits, which was great. It also meant that employees of low rank such as me had again worked miracles at making rich men richer. I had diligently worked for the same company for over three years and had not seen a single dime of increase on my salary. I was in charge of what some might call the bulk of their business activities, their client base. I was responsible for over 300 of them, making sure that our software systems and products were doing what they were designed to do and helping the clients with any related issues.

My clients could attest to my dedication, integrity and a job well done with at least a 98 percent satisfaction rating. When the management could no longer ignore me, they unanimously decided to give me a high-performance award, which came with a congratulatory letter and a $50 gift certificate. They also gave me a small piece of the pie—a bonus that was a one-time check in the amount of just over $800 for the entire fiscal year. This is in light of the fact that I, along with colleagues like myself, through hard work, literally made the company millions of dollars in profit. I should have been happy and thankful for getting some kind of recognition, which I was, as not everyone was as fortunate in that area as me.

We were underpaid, overworked, did most of the heavy lifting and still scraped by financially, barely surviving. Mister Duck Mushier closed his nice little speech by proudly and jokingly saying a farewell to one of the managers who was promoted to a higher managerial post, requiring him to move to the company headquarters located in a different state. As he put it while looking at him with a funny smile, "The only other thing separating him and us now is the long drive." To this, everyone laughed and applauded at the same time.

At the beginning of each of the picnic parties, as it has been in the past three years, everyone was given a raffle ticket for a possible prize at the end of the event. The raffle in my opinion was an unambiguous design to force people to stay throughout the entire event. It worked for the most part, but Katrina had also warned us that we would be having a talk with her the next day, if any of us dared to leave early anyway. And no one in their right mind wanted to have that kind of talk with her. Katrina, understandably, wanted her and her department to have the best possible impression on the company's upper management team. Who could blame her? She was just promoted to a higher paying and much more demanding upper manager role, where everyone in her group knew she was not even good enough for the lower post she would be leaving behind. The way some of us saw it, leaving early would soon be the least of her concerns. Katrina's career path was not my judgment to call; besides, I was trying to get back on her good side, so I obeyed and did not leave early.

Soon enough, the organizer, announced the beginning of the games. We all needed to mix and form different teams of four to five individuals. The goal was to have each team compete against each other trying to answer random trivia questions the best way we could. The team with the highest correct responses would win and get a random prize. My team didn't win, and I was happy with that. I was less motivated to participate, and the team lacked motivation and a sense of excitement—something I could have easily provided, but did not. My heart just was not in it from the very start.

After the game, everyone was asked to get up for a physical activity, where we needed to toss feather-like balloons into some colorful, flat, circular baskets; easier said than done. The balloons were so light; no amount of force was enough to land them exactly where we wanted them to land. Applying too much force did not help. To win, one must be gentle with the ball and thoughtful about elements such as the height at which the ball was released and the speed and direction of the wind. That was a graceful moment, and at the same time, a great challenge. It also was my favorite activity of the day; it was fun and offered a moment as light as the balloons we were trying to land in the flat, circular baskets. A long moment later, Jennifer announced the moment we all had been waiting: the raffle tickets to mark the end of the afternoon.

Jennifer also stated that she was going to do things a little differently. Instead of reading the ticket numbers from the number one prize, to the number three prize. She was going to read the tickets from the descending order starting, from the number three down. There were about thirty people at the picnic, and only three were going to be rewarded for participating; fair enough. This certainly should not take a lot of time, I figured, since I could not wait to go home. I also figured that I did not want to win, because it would have made me more memorable. But I didn't need to worry about that; the odds were against me anyway. Considering that I had not won anything in a very long time, a lot of people actually wanted me to win. I was somewhat positive, and I was about to get my wish granted. As Jennifer plunged her right hand in the basket full of small, blue raffle tickets and grabbed one, I held my breath.

She then adjusted her glasses and started to read the numbers one at the time. Jennifer read the entire sequence of numbers, paused for a few seconds, and then looked around as if to scan the faces for the winner. She didn't find any; and then I thought I heard her reading the winning number for what seemed the second or he third time. That was when I remembered to put my hand in my pocket and felt my ticket, pulled it out and started to pay attention. Sure enough, I was the first winner. I quietly raised my hand high with the winning ticket between my fingers, to a big round of applause. I hoped no one was actually looking at me, but I knew that was nearly impossible. Unbelievable! I had won something. I had won the microfiber blanket embroidered with the company logo—probably the most memorable prize of the night. I went up to get my prize and was handed a piece of paper. The prize, I was told, wasn't there yet. It had been ordered and would be delivered to my work address in a few days.

David, my coworker with whom I was standing, won the third prize, which was supposed to be the first, since the order was reversed. He won a lunch for the entire department with the company's vice president, Mister Duck Mushier. But Mister Duck Mushier could not make it to the lunch with our team because of other engagements, and I wasn't surprised. Because of that, the responsibility fell onto none other than Katrina to take us to lunch at her convenience. A short while later, Mister Duck Mushier openly congratulated the winners, myself included.

The picnic ended on that note, and we all helped with the cleaning. The leftover food was there for the taking on a first-come, first-serve basis. Whatever could not be taken away was thrown in the trash. I helped clean the place, but I was in no way interested in taking any food home. I just could not wait to get out of there, and fast. The event I did not want to attend had come and gone like it did not really take place. I found myself driving home and wondering what just happened. There I was almost hiding in plain sight, not wanting to draw any attention to myself, and out of nowhere I got called forward to stand in front of everybody to be congratulated for winning a prize I did not want to win. I cannot recall ever winning anything of any significance before in my life; why would this one make any difference? This couldn't be a mere coincidence; I had a feeling there was a hidden message of some sort. I said a little prayer and tried to forget about the entire day.

About two days after the event, I called my little brother Emanuel, who casually asked me how the picnic went. I told him it went well; I also told him that I was a lucky winner of a nice blanket with the company name embroidered on it. To that tune, he exclaimed as if he was punched in the stomach. "Dee, do you realize what that means?" he asked me while wanting me to repeat the story again. "Repeat that again," he said a couple of times in the row, as if he needed some time to decode a secret message.

"No, I don't really know what it means," I said. "But I think it is something good, right?"

He responded convincingly, almost yelling at me through the phone: "Something good ... This here is more than something good; in fact, it is better than something great." He kept going. "This is something wonderful. This is your sign, my brother, a sign that God is on our side. Are you following me?"

"Yes I am following," I said disconcertedly.

"This is a call for celebration; God loves you, man." Emanuel continued, "In my opinion, that was God's way of presenting you to everyone out there, some of whom have already made up their minds about how they feel about you. I think and sincerely believe God was trying to tell them that you are under his shield, his protection, and that you are going to be alright. Come on, man, think about it." Then he momentarily stopped, as if to get my full attention, then continued. "You said you won a blanket, right?"

"Right"

"In your right mind, what do you think is the purpose of a blanket if not to protect someone from the elements? There, my brother, is the sign you have been waiting for."

"Wow, when you put it like that—" But Emanuel wouldn't let me finish my sentence.

"What do you mean, when I put it like that? I did not put anything like anything, okay? It is what it is. You take it or you leave it, but in your case you don't have any choice; God's grace is upon you whether you like it or not. A blanket is a blanket, but not always. This one is not just any other blanket; this is a sign. It just is what it is. You may not understand it, but you cannot change it. This blanket you have won is very much symbolic. Do you understand?"

"Yes, I do, and thank you. But wow, I didn't look at it like that before." I thought to myself. I, a mere humble human, had found favor in the eyes of God Almighty. What had I done to deserve God's mercy? What had I done to deserve his grace? Is that what happens when God decides to show his mercy to someone? As if

I couldn't stop thinking, I heard my brother saying something through the phone.

"God loves you, man. His grace and mercy are upon you; blessed be his Holy name."

"Blessed be his Holy name," I responded.

Then we hung up the phones. At that very moment, my entire body was covered with goosebumps, and a sudden chill traversed my body from my head through my spine and almost freezing my feet to the floor. I suddenly felt cold and almost unable to move. I managed to slowly get myself from the living room to my bedroom and crashed onto the bed. My head completely emptied while my tear-filled eyes wallowed across the ceiling. Not sure about what to do next, I got down on my knees by the side of the bed and whispered a thanksgiving prayer, thanking God for his love and grace and blessing him for remembering me and for showing me his favor and kindness.

CHAPTER 6

The Imminent Danger

Before a Cobra Strikes - It Tastes the Air

Ever since I realized I was an object of demonic attacks, my work life hadn't been the same. I finally concluded this after a series of bad dreams, in addition to an incident involving a flock of crows visiting my workplace right above my head, among other things. While this took me a long while to realize, I immediately froze the minute that happened. I thought about it for a few minutes before deciding what to do. Since I didn't have many options, I did the next best thing and tried to be cautious. My guard went up, as I treaded lightly with everyone in the office, especially Sally Voursheer and Katrina Jones. The last thing I wanted was to give any of them a reason to unleash on me whatever it was they had prepared for me. The fact that they both hated me for reasons beyond my control didn't help my case in their eyes. I couldn't care less. I neither wanted nor expected any favor or approval from any of them. If Sally and Katrina deliberately chose to hate me, it was on them. While I didn't want to share in that grievance, I certainly didn't want to give them any motive with which to have me destroyed. As far as I was concerned, they already had me locked on their radar anyway. I was just determined not to let them demolish me.

A great man of God by the name of Pastor Jeremy Goods, who once anointed my head with oil and spoke blessing words upon my life, spoke to me while I was seated in his congregation. Pastor Goods said: "There were only two ways the evil one can get to us and attack us: one way is through circumstances, and the other way is through people." Pastor Goods also said to "resist, resist and resist, and the evil one would flee." Resist was what I did. Although difficult, resisting to fall into temptation, to yield to something wicked, evil and immoral, and to give up on life was what we must all do when faced with life's seasons and events we would rather do without. The key to winning any battle is, in part, knowing with whom you are dealing. The answer to that question can help determine what to expect or not to expect. It would also help plot a winning strategy. The battle of life is no different.

The only noticeable difference is that most of the time we have no idea with whom or what we are dealing; and that is a major problem. When that happens, we have the choice of taking things into our own hands or run. I chose God, and invited him to take precedence over my life, my fight and everything else that was near and dear to me. I consider myself blessed and grateful to be in this position to share my story, my testimony with you today. My only hope is to help you and to continue to fight a good battle in God who has called us to be strong and courageous as it is written:

> "Have not I commanded you? Be strong and of a good courage; be not afraid, neither be you dismayed: for the LORD your God is with you wherever you go"
> —Joshua 1:9 (King James Version)

This passage will help and guide you through every single one of your unique life's situations, however daunting or dire they may appear.

All we need to do to win the fight, any fight in reality, is to humble ourselves and pray. While this might sound idiotic and counterintuitive; trust me, it works. This is because any good battle is often won before it actually begins, at the planning and preparation stages. Letting God take control trumps any type of planning; it is the most effective type of strategy. Victory is but a sure thing. After that, all we need to do is to resist temptations from various shapes and forms and stay strong. Above all, we need to pray without ceasing; this has worked wonders for me.

While things may appear difficult, and they often are, our battles are never ours to fight alone, especially the battle against dark spirits. It was God's, as he would level the playing field and give us a fighting chance. Without that, we are honestly doomed. Why would anyone in his right mind go up against an enemy far too sinister and far too powerful, alone? This proverbial battle of good versus evil has been around from the very beginning of time, and no one could actually avoid it. There is no running or hiding from it.

All we can try to do is avoid it, but even that doesn't work. Knowing this, why would anyone want to physically fight a spiritual battle? It has always been my understanding that spiritual things should be handled spiritually; and since God is a spirit, praying to him in spirit alone addressed that part of the equation. Praying to God in spirit is not a game or a joke; it is a very crucial and systematic fighting strategy.

I have long learned that keeping the body, mind, spirit and soul strong is virtually a prerequisite to having a good prayer life, which is a prerequisite to winning a fight against the evil one, assuming you too want to win a fight over the evil one. A fervent prayer from a pure heart has always been a formidable apparatus against any enemy or enemies, however small, big, powerful and bloodcurdling they may be. It works. This also has worked for me in the past. Anyone who understands the power of prayers is expected to know this.

Sally led the charge with some random and false accusatory statements about random projects. At first, it seemed she was trying to get me to say something so she could accuse me. This only caused me to be even more careful around her. I wouldn't and didn't insult or say anything wrong to her directly or in any of our email correspondences. But it didn't really matter whether I denounced her claims or simply provided the correct information; I was wrong, and I was guilty without any type of hearing. A response was what she really wanted, and that was something I didn't know ahead of time. Had I known this, I wouldn't have said anything, and so played directly into her hands. Sally sent me emails and accused me of something, or twisted my own words regarding any random project or work-related issue, and secretly catalogued my responses. If I responded and corrected her, I was wrong. If I did not respond I was also wrong because then she would use the false information to make me look bad. This was going on because she knew Katrina, our local departmental manager, who was promoted to the general manager role, had been too incapacitated to fairly mediate any dispute or misunderstanding without taking Sally's side. This was obvious, and it had gotten to the point where talking to Katrina in most cases was a waste of time.

So even though I needed help with Sally's situation, I kept to myself. After careful consideration, I opted to answer some of Sally's emails with detailed explanations. In fact, Katrina told me to do so to avoid miscommunication and to clarify information after every mandatory meeting. Now looking back at things, I should have reached out to HR and should never have actually played into Sally's hand by exchanging emails with her. No matter how harmless my emails were at explaining specific work-related projects by providing details, data and traceable information to support my ideas, they were always offensive to Sally. Sally labeled and catalogued them. It had gotten to a point where I became frustrated for having to repeat myself, and stopped responding to her emails entirely. That too did not work so well; Sally labeled that "ignoring her," apparently a much graver offence.

Sally would come to the office dressed in mostly all black, walking on the tip of her toes, with arrogance, while leaning forward. This made her look like she was almost walking on air, with her long trench coat catching the air and making her look like a character straight out of a vampire movie. Her feet were barely touching the ground. This was a blond-haired white lady in her mid-50s. Could this be her version of a midlife crisis, a way to try to relive her adolescence? What was she trying to prove? Who was she trying to intimidate? If that was her intent, she would have to do more than that. Little did I know, she did just that when she made it her mission to ruin me.

I decided to put a distance between myself and Sally. She, in turn, decided to confront me. One day, I thought I overheard her just a few feet away from the direction of the hallway, quickly approaching my cubicle; my senses were up and I could actually sense an impending confrontation. But before Sally could step into my cubicle, I quickly turned around to meet her with my eyes, stopping her dead at the entrance of the cube, as if I had been waiting for her all along. She stopped for a moment, took a second to catch her breath, and then proceeded.

"Dee, I have noticed you no longer interact with me like before, and I want to let you know that I do not like it," Sally said to me in a quarrelsome manner. Obviously she had a problem with me trying to distance myself from her. But wasn't she the one constantly sabotaging me and provoking me with random accusatory emails? I was confused. What did she want this time—to force me into saying something she could turn around and use against me?

"Oh really, and what makes you think that?" I calmly responded, still seated and directly locking eyes with her, tracking her every breath. Anyone could tell Sally came with an intention to give me a serious beating; it was written all over her. But she either wasn't sure how to deliver her blows, or I was just too much for her to handle.

"Well, ever since we have talked about the project "John Doe," your attitude toward me has significantly changed."

"Are you sure?"

"Yes, I am, and—" She was nearly screaming at me. Seeing where she was going, I immediately interrupted her and didn't let her finish her sentence. I caught her right when her voice suddenly reached peak volume.

"You are raising your voice at me!" I quickly and peacefully stated as if unfazed by her intimidation.

"Oh, you think I'm yelling at you now? Let's go for a meeting to address this!" Then she started heading in the opposite direction to her cube. Not knowing where she was heading, I quickly responded.

"I am busy; I will let you know when I have a few minutes to meet." At this, she stopped, and without adding a single word, she slowly changed directly and turned back, passing by my cube to hers.

Who did this lady think she was? I didn't mind the way she was talking to me, but it was still our workplace. I knew she must have had some devious plans. I just couldn't tell how devious they were. Under normal circumstances, I would have gone to Katrina right away, told her what was going on, and hoped that she would at least do something about it; but this wasn't a normal circumstance. From all I could think, Sally might have been emboldened by Katrina to take whatever action she thought fitting against me; after all, they both wanted to kill me. This was bad.

If Sally was trying to frighten me, she failed. But why was she heading in the wrong direction? Was she trying to take me to the parking lot outside for an actual physical altercation, or to beat me into worshipping her? Why would she take me to the back where there would be virtually no witnesses? I didn't trust Sally before, and I certainly did not trust her now. It became clear to me at a much later time that Sally really intended to mess me up—that is to say, destroy me. Who knew what she had planned to do to me had I followed her, alone, in the back office where no one could actually hear our voices?

My company occupied two floors with a total of five conference rooms. Three conference rooms were located on the first floor, while two were on the second floor where my department was located. The biggest conference room where a large group of employees, about 40-plus people, could meet was on the first floor. Our regular team meetings were usually hosted in the smaller second-floor conference room, which was directly facing my cubicle. We occasionally used the second conference room located in the far back corner of the office floor for bigger departmental meetings. We did this rarely, and only for special occasions, like when we had visitors, usually from the company headquarters. That was also the only time we had team meals on the company, usually consisting of pizza, chicken wings and soda, to commemorate a major business venture or after long mandatory training sessions.

It turned out that was where Sally was trying to have me isolated for her so-called meeting with me. Following her would have been the same as cutting off my own head and handing it to her on a platter. While I did not really want to meet with her, I felt it was necessary. After all, I would not want her to be singing about it and telling people how I refused to sit down with her to figure out a solution to our deteriorating working relationship. That would have been making things too easy for her. Had I indeed refused to meet with Sally, all she needed to do was to say that I had refused to help work on our deteriorating work relationship affecting business productivity. That was that; and I would be in a serious trouble. So I agreed to meet sometime Friday; that would have been three days from the day since she barged into my cubicle, looking for a fight.

On the day of the meeting, there were not many people in our department. Only I, Sally and David, our other colleague, were at work that day. Unsurprisingly enough, many people tended to request Fridays off to have an extended three-day weekend. I was as calm as the surface of a body of water. The only difference was that my senses were purposely heightened and amplified even days leading up to the meeting. Ever since Sally had been trying to get me in trouble, I had figuratively grown a pair of eyes on the back of my head and on each of my shoulders. I had become so in sync with my surroundings that I could tell if someone, and in some cases who was walking behind me without the need to turn around and look at the person. That was how I was able to answer Sally just a day after I refused to follow her to the back conference room, the day she actually yelled at me in her attempt to terrorize me. If mere looks could kill, Sally would have killed me a long time ago.

Sure enough, Sally once again was trying to take me to the far back end conference room. And she was actually expecting me to follow her, when I quickly stopped her: "Where are you going?" I asked. Without giving her a chance to respond, I added, "We can meet here." I then pointed to the small conference room where we usually met. In fact, we never ever had any one-on-one meeting in the far back end conference room before in the entire three and a half years I had been working at the company. It always was either at her desk, my desk, or the small conference room. At this, she stopped dead and confused. I could tell she knew something was off, as my eyes were again tracking her every move and constantly sizing her up. My blood was already literally boiling hot, as if faced with an eminent danger. As I was ready for the worst, I could swear if I had an ice block in my hand, it would have melted instantly. I was fighting my hardest just to control my temper, my breath, just to come across as civil, as polite and as peaceful as I possibly could.

I knew with absolute certainty that Sally could not take me on in a physical fight and win. She would have been a fool to even attempt such a thing. But if she was desperate, and so dying to isolate me, it would have to be for one or two reasons: One, so she could try some of her magic spells on me, since she hated me that much and she might have been into dark magic or even witchcraft. For all I knew, she could have been a witch. And Sally was running the risk of exposing herself. Two, so she could have me mugged or beaten up by a group of people she might have paid to teach me some lesson. Option two was less likely because I would never in a million years follow her outside to the parking lot area. Having me mugged within the company premises would have resulted in a massive lawsuit against her and the company. Before she could make it to the smaller conference room, Sally called out, "David." I knew right away what she was trying to do. She was resorting to a cover-up; what was a better way to say she wasn't what I thought she was the entire time? It was very clever of her to invite someone else to listen in the meeting.

A few minutes later, David showed up. "Is everything alright?" he asked. Sally was the one who called David, so I let her answer that question.

"Yes, David. Can you please sit in a meeting with Dee and me?" she asked in a demanding voice as if she owned both David and his time. I could have cared less.

"I guess I could," responded David confusedly, not knowing exactly what was going on.

"*Poor David …*" I kept thinking to myself, "*poor David*". Deep down I was glad he got to witness whatever would not happen next. That was to say, Sally would have resorted to her second plan, because she knew I was highly suspicious of her, which would have been an understatement. I waited for Sally, then David, to sit down before I sat in the opposite side of the table to Sally. David awkwardly sat down at far right-hand corner of the table with his back to the door. He wanted to know what was going on, and if we really needed him there.

"Hey guys, what is going on?" he asked again, in an amusing voice; and I was assuming he wasn't too pleased to be dragged from whatever he was working on to join an unscheduled meeting.

"Not much is going o—" But before I completed that sentence, Sally jumped in:

"We will be pleased if you listen in on this meeting for us," Sally sarcastically added. Then I thought to myself, didn't she say that already? What was going on with this lady?

"I would like Dee to start and let us know why his attitude toward me personally has changed so much in the past couple of months."

This whole thing seemed so unprofessional. I pulled my hand out of my pocket; in it, was my smart phone. I then discretely pressed the record button to record our conversation, before placing the phone on the table in front of me. My honest reply to Sally's inquiry would have been "seriously?" But I knew better not to give her an honest reply. From what I was able to see, there was nothing honest about that meeting, so I would just play along. Looking at both Sally and David, I started.

"I don't really know what you mean, but if you think you have noticed a change in my demeanor toward you, it probably was because of three reasons. One, because of the project John Doe, you wrongfully have tried to force me to take a fall for doing my job well; you have pushed me under the bus. Did you realize that? And two, because you came to my cubicle and yelled at me while all I was trying to do was go about doing my daily job peacefully. Did you hear yourself? You yelled at me, at work … And three, you shut me off during the team meeting just a couple of weeks ago while I was trying to get a point across." My heart and my nerves were still fighting to jump out of me. It took me a great deal of strength to keep my voice steady and to stay as calm as possible. I refused to give in.

"Was that all?" Sally nervously asked, hoping that I would spill the beans about what I knew, she knew, I knew she was. The truth of the matter was Sally was no ordinary sweet old lady; she had people believe she was. She was not just a wife, a mother and a grandmother. While I may not know exactly what or who she was, she had been messing with some dark and evil spirit with intent to harm. *"Oh! not me. She couldn't harm me."* If my intuitions were right, she was a dark sorceress at the very least; but she wouldn't hear that from me. That was the object of this plan B meeting, since I refused to follow her to my death, to the isolation in the other conference room where she had certainly prepared something sinister for me.

"Well, if that was the way you felt then I am sorry," she quickly said, and that was about the end of the meeting she had been itching to have with me for nearly a week.

"Seriously?" I quietly said to myself without realizing that she could actually hear my voice.

"Yes Dee! Seriously; what do you want me to do? Do you want me to apologize to you in front of everyone at our next team meeting?" Sally quickly added in a defying tone as if to say, "You have no idea what I am capable of doing."

I almost said yes to that proposition because a part of me really wanted to see how she would pull that off, and then I quickly caught myself. This could be a trap, as she could very well spin things out of proportion to make me look like the bad guy. Besides, I was already tired of her and would have wished to be left alone. I just wanted to have a peaceful work environment again.

"Oh no; nothing. Please, you don't need to apologize to me," I directly responded, keeping eye contact with her and David. As if they didn't hear me the first time, I added on a serious note, "I don't think you should do anything else. Thank you."

That was it; that was the bulk of the meeting. After that, we talked for a few minutes about random things, with no substance, as Sally was trying to get into my mind to see what I knew and what I was going to do about it. I could actually see her as a hungry shark circling me and waiting for a blood drop, which I wasn't willing to provide.

"Dee, but you have changed, and your voice—" I didn't want her to complete that sentence because I knew my voice wasn't perfect. I also knew that I spoke with some accent from being born in a different country, and having lived there in my early childhood.

"I know my voice isn't perfect, but this is me. This is who I am and how I talk."

"Nope, I've known you for some time now, and that right there is not your normal voice." I didn't want to answer that question, so I shook my shoulders as if to say, "Says you!"

Maybe she was right. My voice wasn't the same. People tend to react under pressure differently. Maybe I wasn't doing such a great job protecting and concealing my inner emotion. There was a tornado of fire raging uncontrollably inside of me; and all I could do was to try my very best to control it as peacefully as possible. Maybe that interfered with my vocal cords, affecting the sound of my voice; or maybe Sally was just saying that to make me doubt and question myself. Either way, she wouldn't hear a sip from me.

"I always thought you guys were great teammates together," said David; who was trying to be a great mediator, and I thought he did a wonderful job. "I always admire the working relationship between everyone in this office. Before I joined the group not too long ago, I did not know you guys were having any problem or any misunderstanding. But I hope you now have put it all behind you." We both thanked David almost at once as he was getting ready to exit the room.

I waited for Sally to follow him before I exited the room last. I thought that was a useless meeting. What the meeting really did was solidify Sally in her wicked desire and conviction to bring me down. That was because she did not get anything out of me. And I definitely did not present her with an opportunity to do to me what she had planned all along. That made her very mad. I was able to clearly see through her that day. Certain things could not be communicated openly; but I was able to read Sally, and would not forget anytime soon what I saw. I knew this was far from over; she was that transparent.

Admittedly, I was not perfect by any means. And, I could have handled the entire situation a lot differently, which could have prevented it from reaching that height. One of my flaws was being very good at purposely dismissing, ignoring, and sometime completely burying both people and problems alike. That is to turn them a deaf ear, not to avoid them; but as a defensive way of dealing with them, and to seal them out. While that imperfection of mine, might have contributed to this problem; I now know that systematically categorizing, or chastising someone as in turning a page on him or her just because they wronged me wasn't at all a way to resolve any issue; of this, I was guilty. There are at least two sides to everyone: a nice side, and a not so nice side – a naughty side like some people like call it. Some people's naughty sides are far worse than others'. I could have gone to Sally in the beginning, and politely seek to talk with her, to earnestly attempt to figure a solution to what was known as our issues. But I didn't, and that was squarely my fault; and something that might have landed me on Sally's naughty side, a place I'd rather not be.

CHAPTER 7

The Going

You Can Never Be Too Careful

There are many unknown elements in life. Surviving any of them is just what it is, "surviving." But undeniably, even that requires a certain level of discipline, a know-how, an art. I did not know how to survive every single one of those obstacles as they happened. But what I did know I desperately tried to apply to the unique situation I was experiencing, knowing full well it would soon be behind me. I wasn't afraid. My heart shook not, for I had faith. Deep down in my heart, I knew at the end I was going to be alright.

If you ever have felt someone hate you so much to the point where you could actually feel and taste it on your breath, then you probably already have an idea of what I was actually going through, dealing with both Sally Voursheer, my colleague, and Katrina Jones, my department manager. They each wanted to make my life miserable, but more than that, they wanted me dead.

Sally and Katrina both, in their own way, tried to set traps for me. I, on the other hand, had made the conscious decision to live my life regardless. My only immediate concern at the time was to self-preserve, to somehow stay as vigilant as I possibly could.

Directly above my cubicle, flocks of crows had begun visiting the roof above the office. Sally asked me about them just a few days later, and this made me very suspicious. That question pushed me to the furthest corner of the already dangling edge of where I was standing. It also made me wonder how committed Sally and Katrina were about taking me out, about killing me. Either way, they couldn't.

This was because I knew my God would not forsake me. It is written:

> "Be strong and of a good courage, fear not, nor be afraid of them: for the LORD your God, He it is that does go with you; He will not fail you, nor forsake you."
> —Deuteronomy 31.6 (King James Version)

So what? I hear you say. But I prayed the black birds away, their symbol of death, near death, and the bad omen of popular belief. I prayed for the Holy Ghost fire of God upon them; and it came to pass. I believed that with all my heart, because they and I had no business in common. The last time I checked, darkness and light just didn't mix together. In fact, Sally confirmed this herself when she talked to me just a couple of days later, as I walked to the cafeteria to get my afternoon coffee: "Dee, what has happened to our birds?" She asked as if I knew something about her evil deeds. I couldn't believe my ears, what I was hearing. Her manner was as blunt and casual as ever, but she had asked the question as if she knew I had something to do with those impure birds' disappearance. Of course, as a matter of fact, I did. So I fervently replied, "Oh, those birds? They were burned!" I might not have seen them physically on fire myself, but it was what I had requested in my prayer. Sally instinctively froze as if she had seen a ghost. She stood still for a few long seconds before proceeding back to her own cubicle, where she hid herself from view for the remainder of the day.

While I couldn't care less, I also knew I shouldn't have replied the way I did. Even if God had answered my prayers, as I believed he had; it was still wrong for me to rub the fact so openly in Sally's face. My ego had gotten the best of me, but I was neither ashamed nor regretful.

Could that declaration of mine mean Sally and her friends would now solicit help from even far more powerful, evil people than themselves to try to subdue me? I could have ignored her, ignored the question, switched the topic of discussion and avoided answering the question altogether; but I hadn't. The last thing I wanted was having evil people gather about me. I knew I should have done better. My answer was a catalyst, designed to produce a response. Thankfully I had a clear and conscious mind and could always see dangers from afar. I only hoped and prayed I was never caught dormant, with my guard down.

Life is too short to doubt our intuition; doing so can come at a cost. That little voice inside our head and in our heart that whispers quietly in our ears is our conscience. Listen to it! It is our ultimate internal ethical compass, and in many cases, a good indicator of our sense of wrong and right. We can call it a moral ethic—an innate code of conduct that keeps us level-headed and in sync with ourselves in the face of the many often confusing and contradicting decisions life has to offer. Call it what you want, but whatever you do please do not so easily disregard it. It could be your inner voice of reason if you let it. For it is in reality the breath of God serving as our very own guide.

We were created in the image of God, after all. And in all of us there must be some absolute good somewhere deep down inside without exception, regardless of who we are or where we come from. That little, subtle voice may have saved me from an ultimate trap—a trap to which I was glad I didn't succumb. There is no possible way for me to prove either way, but my heart has never lied to me. So I listened, and was at peace with my conscience. I would rather choose to listen and be wrong than not listen at all, still be wrong and pay a stiff price.

Just like when a storm is slowly building, we can tell: We see the wind turning and picking up speed, the clouds gathering, changing color and formation. Soon after we instinctively know that the rain will not be too far behind. I too felt the same, and I took notice when my surrounding situation was changing for the worse. The company embroidered blanket I had won at the company picnic not too long ago? Well, it was delivered to me with a little spin.

It was Sally, the very same coworker I have seen in my dream on two occasions. Each time she has appeared in the form of a snake, and was associating herself with snakes that wanted to bite me. Out of all people, she had to be the one to bring me my blanket. After all, this wasn't just any blanket. It was, according to my brother Emanuel, whom we nicknamed the pastor because of his zeal for anything God-related, a symbol representative of God's protection, and his grace toward me in particular. Emanuel explained that we use blankets to protect ourselves from the elements, and there was the correlation. I believed and trusted Emanuel on his words that God was in my corner. Sally intercepting my blanket couldn't possibly have been a coincidence, nor could it have been an accident. If the little voice inside my head and my heart was right, it was a deliberate and calculated move—one more subtle ruse from Sally in her attempt to get me.

The company picnic I hadn't really wanted to attend quickly came and went. Most people had fun; I painfully held my breath through the entire occasion because my heart wasn't in it. Although the majority of the event was damp and soaked in rain, it wasn't anything we hadn't seen before. In fact, the reservation email clearly stated, "rain or shine, the party will go on." In a way, everyone was warned, even though a sunny and a magnificently clear and dazzling blue sky was to be expected that time of the year. It was summer, after all. I, on the other hand, have learned that winning a microfiber blanket at that venue, in that particular time of my life (I was feeling threatened, unappreciated and oppressed), and in that particular manner (being called in front of everyone and congratulated when I least expected it) was a sign of God's favor toward me. That day at work, while the day was slowly and painfully dripping away as it had been for the past few months, and I was trying to solve some of my usual work assignments in my cubicle, I was interrupted by a familiar noise. It was Sally, fast approaching my cubicle.

Before I could turn around and look up, there she was, standing at the entrance of my cubicle with something in her hand.

"Hello, Dee, I think you have a package," Sally said at the entrance of my cubicle with a smirk on her face.

"A package? What package?" I slowly said, trying to think about who could possibly send me a package at work. I had never given my work address to anyone I knew. Without saying a word, Sally stretched her arms toward me. In her arms was a light, green-looking fleece blanket, neatly tied together with an organic, decorative cord. "Thank you."

Without a single word, Sally disappeared back into her cubicle. Perplexed, I quickly said a prayer and blessed the blanket; but even that did not appease my conscience. At home, I showed the blanket to my family, but forbade any of them from touching it. I then placed the blanket in a plastic bag, tied it up, and put it away in the storage room of my apartment building in the basement, before eventually giving it away to a local Goodwill store. It was only then that I felt some sense of harmony with the little voice inside my heart. Sally was conniving, and I didn't have to know what she did to the blanket to know she did something to it. The fact that the blanket was a symbolic representation of God's grace toward me and not the actual grace made it easy for me to let it go.

Katrina might be the office manager, but Sally had her exactly where she wanted her, wrapped all around her pointing finger, to control and to manipulate. Either way, I was convinced they were both working together with some sort of dark spirit, with Sally obviously being the spiritually stronger of the two. Together, they were a bad and grimy mixture. Their resentment toward me, and others like me, was just a byproduct. Fortunately, this was revealed to me, and I was on my guard. They couldn't take me down. I couldn't be so ignorant as to let them destroy me; no one in his right mind has ever laid down his own life to anyone he knew ahead of time hated him, by being careless around them. And I wasn't going to be the first. Sally and her friends were hugely mistaken if that was what they were expecting. I knew I was a different specimen, for I was a child of God. My grandmother didn't raise a fool; my God couldn't possibly have created a thoughtless me. I may have been momentarily shocked and stunned, but I would not succumb to any of them; that much I knew.

In fact, I sincerely believed people who believed in God and his promises have a certain characteristic that set them apart from everyone else. That is, they actually have hope, a promise of a better turnaround, and maybe an actual earthly better future. For one, they don't react in the face of danger the way everyone else does. They have reasons to be calm and collected. In a way, they are natural-born winners, created brave and courageous in the image of the true and living God. As I have heard many times before, the only way, and time, the evil one was going to prevail over them was when they actually let it, one way or another. When we knowingly give up the fight, we lower our arms and surrender to sinful ways and situation; we are unconsciously allowing the evil one to rule over us – thus condemning us. Once condemned, the downfall is but imminent. I have long made a conscious decision not to let that happen to me, hopefully not ever again. If I ever find myself slipping, I can always run to God the Father and find favor in his abundant grace.

As it turned out, Katrina, who had been looking for her replacement to take over her local managerial responsibilities, had finally found herself a suitable match. Since she has been promoted to the company-wide general manager role; It was in Katrina's best interest to find and hire a local manager to take over her previous position. The employment agencies and other hiring managers helping her had unsuccessfully tried to recruit a few good candidates in the past. There had been a few unsuccessful interviews, but most notably there was this great candidate Katrina was so thrilled about and really wanted to hire. After the candidate had successfully gone through the interview process and was actually offered the job, he turned it down just a couple of days before the start date. The candidate had sent Katrina the infamous "sorry, no can do" email without further explanation. Katrina was so furious. She would have loved to bring the candidate back in the office just so she could be able to fire him herself, to teach him a lesson. How did I know these things? Katrina told us herself during one of our meetings. After that, another candidate did a similar thing before this new and most recent candidate finally agreed to take the job to Katrina's delight. Whether the salary, the job responsibilities, or the workplace ambiance had spooked the earlier candidates away was something no one would probably ever know.

The great news was that someone actually accepted the offer to join Katrina's group, without the need to bail out at the end. That was factually more than great news; to Katrina, it was literally liberating news, as she would finally be set to assume bigger and better things as the general manager. So ever since we were given the news, Katrina just couldn't wait to fully embrace her new position and couldn't stop talking about the new hire. We didn't have much of a choice but to wait and meet our new manager. A day had been set, and the new hire would soon be starting. Life at the office remained the same, while time seemed to have gone by faster every day. There still was an invisible tension in the air.

Colleagues didn't make small talks anymore. Everyone kept to himself. No one, not even Katrina, dared to do anything about it. This was also a situation everyone had grown to ignore, minding their own business. I, along with everyone else, have learned to avoid causing any type of friction with anyone by staying in my own lane. Things were great that way. After all, I was the one with a job to lose should anything stir. Then there was this question of a coinciding matching paid leave request between Sally and me, which Katrina seemed to be having a very hard time sorting out. Other than that, everything else appeared exquisite in the office, to the outside world.

In light of Sally consistently getting the Friday after Thanksgiving off, I consciously refuse to roll over this time around. I simply couldn't resist the idea of not standing for my right at least once in my life. It was a matter of principle, and nothing more. This, however, didn't sit well with Katrina, and of course Sally. Expectedly, almost the entire office would be out that day as they were last year and the year before that, leaving me working all by myself. While my duty required my presence, I didn't think it was fair to me. I was a low-paid support analyst, not the CEO. While the company couldn't afford to have everyone off on a popular day, it was the manager's job to balance the schedule for every employee, and not just the ones Katrina liked. Katrina had a major decision to make, and I didn't really care which way she went. I just hoped she made the right decision.

Katrina told me during our most recent one-on-one scheduled meeting, " … It is only fair you too [referring to me after I brought up the issue] get this Friday after Thanksgiving off." That was all I needed to hear. Whether Sally worked on that same day or not was none of my concern. But when I realized Katrina didn't approve my request on the team calendar the Wednesday before Thanksgiving, I suspected something was not right. As a result, I didn't call; I didn't even send her an email like I would have normally done, no! I personally walked straight into her office unannounced, and uninvited.

"Hi Katrina, I am truly sorry for the interruption."

"Hi Dee, what's up?"

"Nothing; I just realized today is Wednesday, and tomorrow would be Thursday, Thanksgiving Day. And you haven't yet approved my request for Friday or Monday on the team calendar," I politely said.

"Oh, really? I have been super busy a lot lately. Thanks for the reminder."

"No problem, and sorry for the interruption."

I walked away feeling a little less nervous than I had been a few minutes earlier, for I thought she would approve my paid leave and everything would be alright. It was past one o'clock in the afternoon, and an email announcement came letting everyone know that we could leave early for the day, courtesy of the upper management. It was customary; and we were all appreciative. They wanted us to leave early to hopefully beat the traffic, since many people were expected to be traveling that day. While I didn't trust Katrina, I was sure walking into her office uninvited and unannounced was the best way not to permit her to play the "I forgot" or "I didn't remember" card. I knew she had a difficult choice to make. Wrong or right, I was just hoping to push her to make an honest one, without any possibility whatsoever of hiding behind anything, not even the probability that she might indeed forget.

I also told Katrina I would be traveling to visit friends and family members, which was a lie on my part. While I didn't plan on traveling anywhere for the holiday, I thought making up that story would have added to my request some much-needed traction. I was wrong. Whether Katrina went back on her words, or was just too afraid of Sally to actually turn down her request instead, Katrina didn't approve my request, and it wasn't because she forgot. It was easier for Katrina to grant Sally's request instead of mine. This is because she was, in fact, afraid of Sally, and I was the easiest target. I have discovered this all on my own.

There was a different facet to Sally's personality most people would rather not know. Katrina must have figured that out at some point. Sally was that sinisterly obvious at times. Katrina was probably, and rightfully, afraid. I definitely understood her difficult position; and it was okay. Sure Katrina told a little white lie, similar to what I did during our most recent meeting; but who was to say it wasn't to save her own skin?

Sure enough, our newest manager, Evelyn, reported for her very first day of work. Her first assignment was to meet the team. How hard could that be? Before Evelyn, our new local departmental manager was even introduced; almost everyone on our office floor already knew she had arrived. Katrina had spoken so highly and so repeatedly of her that the expectation was high. Almost everyone wanted to meet her. Her arrival that morning was echoing, buzzing and slowly moving upward from the first floor, as would locusts when moving together in ranks. Yes! It was that vibrant. Evelyn first arrived at the first floor office, as did every visitor, and met with the receptionist, who greeted her joyfully, because who wouldn't? The receptionist took her picture on the spot to make her personnel badge, which was a security photo ID card every employee must have to access the building. She then gave the new manager her interim badge that did not have any photo, to use until her personal badge was delivered a few days later. The receptionist finally called Katrina to come escort her own, personal, handpicked replacement.

Katrina was eager, happy and so proud to have acquired Evelyn. She happily greeted Evelyn with a warm hug and expressed how glad she was that Evelyn has joined the company. Knowing Katrina, the conversation would have gone something like the following.

"Hey there, how are you? Great to see you again! You didn't have any issue parking your car; did you find the place alright? Is there anything I can help you with …?" Katrina proceeded to be as cordial as possible.

"I am good, thank you. How about you? I had no problem parking, and the place isn't too far, so no, I didn't have any problem finding it at all. Good to see you too!" reciprocated Evelyn with a wide smile. After the greeting, Katrina immediately accompanied Evelyn to meet the team.

Without wasting any time, she started to give Evelyn a quick tour of the office, starting with the first floor. The time was around 10 AM, and most people were already at work and at their desk. Both Evelyn and Katrina chatted candidly, as would two old friends, as they went about from one office space—whether it was an actual office room or a cubicle—to another. Each employee was informed ahead of time of Evelyn's arrived and was almost ordered to be nice, to briefly introduce themselves and to make Evelyn feel welcomed. Everyone hoped she felt welcomed; I certainly did. But again, if Evelyn was anyone like me, she would have felt welcomed right out of the gate and pleased with her decision to join the company, because those bills stacking up at the end of each month were not going to pay themselves.

The job might not have been ideal, but it paid the bills. Working there wasn't so much about self-worth, personal achievement or any sense of life's accomplishment at all. It was about being able to keep up with the bills at the end of the month, plain and simple. I didn't even get the chance to deploy my entire arsenal of technical skillsets or potential. I was given neither the platform nor the necessary incentive to even begin that process. But already, I couldn't wait to move on. Working there, as in finding a lifetime of worthiness or fulfillment, as in something worth doing that brings me joy, was not the case; it was almost deplorable. The opposite, which was not having a job, wasn't what I wanted; it wasn't the best way to go about that issue. So yes, I felt very welcomed! But, Evelyn wasn't me, and so I didn't really know how she felt on her very first day at work. I probably would never have been able to tell what she felt, whether she had made the right choice joining us or not. Either way, we were happy to have her join our team.

It didn't take long before Katrina and Evelyn ran out of rooms to visit on the first floor; as a result, they naturally progressed to the second floor. They both walked up the wide staircase after crossing the big lobby. Katrina swiped the ID badge, enabling them to open the door and enter the second floor office space. Their first stop was Evelyn's own office. It was the very first office from the front main entrance door to the second floor. Located in the corridor leading to the cubicle farm where the rest of us were, Evelyn's office didn't seem to have been used for a great while. This was because it wasn't necessarily what we would call the best location; the foot traffic entering and leaving the floor was a huge distraction. Keeping the office door open wasn't the smartest thing to do. There was a second entrance to the second floor located in the back of the building, which actually led to the back door most people didn't use unless they parked their cars in the back of the building. In spite of its location, Evelyn's office was actually very nice with a lot of room to offer.

It had been exquisitely cleaned and mounted with a new laptop computer on a duck station connected to two large LCD flat-screen monitors. One keyboard and one computer mouse were strategically placed in front of it, and almost at equidistance to the monitors. It was a nice setup. If it weren't for its location, the office would arguably have been the best and probably the ideal office space for anyone in the entire building. After introducing Evelyn to her office, Katrina did the next best thing by allowing Evelyn to get acquainted with her office before meeting the group for our daily stand-up meeting only 30 minutes away. Those eager and audacious enough to want to meet the new manager went to her room and introduced themselves before our daily stand-up. Sally went; I didn't.

At the daily stand-up meeting, we each would have the opportunity to meet our new manager and briefly talk about our respective assignment, as was customary. It was a software development methodology aspect incorporated into our office culture, enabling us to each briefly not only talk about projects we were working on and any new development, but also inform the team about any foreseeable roadblock we might need addressed. But because of Evelyn, Katrina told us the meeting was going to be conducted slightly differently. Instead of talking entirely about projects, we each would be talking more about ourselves, something I hated to do, and less about the project. It was a great way to briefly shine a spotlight on ourselves, and so giving Evelyn an opportunity to get to know us on more or less a personal level.

My first impressions of Evelyn, when we all finally got the chance to meet her for the very first time, were heartwarming and positive. I only prayed she would survive the place. This is because I knew she was going to be tested from many different angles. Standing at approximately five foot five, Evelyn had a nice petite frame, short hairs, brown eyes, and a nice little dress to accommodate both her slender figure, and her smile. She was obviously young, in her mid to late 30, nice, and beautiful at the same time. Strangely enough, Evelyn looked like a younger version of Katrina in appearance, with the only difference being Evelyn was younger, more beautiful, lean, and in a greater physical shape than Katrina. At first glance, Evelyn looked fragile, as though she could have benefited from a couple pounds of body weight and maybe a few inches in height. Evelyn looked like the type that would feel the need to constantly prove to everyone the contrary just to be taken seriously.

This made me wonder if she was going to be able to stand the test of time. On the plus side, she looked and sounded smart. That was good. However, being smart, alone, wasn't enough to survive our kind of work environment at the time; one also needed to have a very thick and resilient skin and an unparalleled physical and mental toughness. I liked Evelyn already, and I wanted her to succeed, and so I made it my mission to support her in my prayers. I sincerely hoped she did not become another casualty in Sally's hands, as the office had a very strict, underlying principle, and an invisible chain of command which placed Sally at the head, and Katrina dangling on strings like a performing puppet at a circus show. If anyone wanted to have a good tenure on the team, it went without saying that he or she should side with Sally regardless of what else might be going on. That was the hidden and often unspoken rule, a rule I refused to follow.

One other thing most people would not know about Sally was, she was also very desperate and would do anything to hold on to her job. Although more quickly approaching retirement than anyone else in the office, Sally hated the idea of retirement. As she once put it, "There is nothing for me to do after I retire. My father worked til he literally dropped dead getting ready to go to work one morning. That is how I feel about work and retirement; work til you drop dead," she once said lightheartedly. But she wasn't joking; she was very serious.

Sally was already over 50 years old, and she wasn't going to let anyone—not even a new manager—get in her way. That office space was her domain, and she had been running things there long before anyone else in that department, even Katrina, was brought in. She had been running the show for over a decade now and planned on continuing to do so many years into the future. And if Katrina was right about what she told us about Evelyn being tough and not backing down for anyone when need be, I could already imagine Evelyn and Sally's clash in the forecast. While she was not physically imposing, Evelyn was athletic, which could easily throw everyone a curve ball and catch anyone who might try to underestimate her by surprise. As an active cyclist, a distance runner and a former track star and coach, I could easily see how Evelyn had both the mental and physical toughness.

"Hello everyone, and please allow me to introduce to you your new local manager, Evelyn. I think I speak for everyone when I say we are very excited to have her joining our team," said Katrina while extending her semi-opened hand in the direction of Evelyn, seated on the right-hand side of the oval conference table. "Welcome to our team." To this, Evelyn flashed a broad smile and muttered between her white and perfectly lined up teeth:

"Thank you for having me."

And the team meeting started. Over the phone were a couple of colleagues who couldn't make it the physical meeting due to the distance, so they dialed in remotely. Over the phone we had Andrew Wallsee, a long-time employee who was calling from Long Island. He too had a chance to welcome our new addition, and wished her good luck. We also had Sophie Elong, another department manager calling in from the company headquarters who happened to oversee Katrina's activities, briefly interjecting into the meeting before leaving for other engagements. As we were all taking turns introducing ourselves as explicitly prescribed by Katrina, something peculiar happened. Everyone was simply asked to state their name, job title and what they actually did. We were also asked to say the name of our college or university, our major and what we liked to do in our spare time; nothing too revealing.

Our department was in charge of the entire company-wide information service's needs. We handled software support, which was to say we handled company-wide information technology issues ranging from application designs, development and implementation and also technical supports. We were a solutions-driven team composed of highly technical individuals. This also explained why our team was a mixture of computer scientists, computer engineers, database administrators and project managers. Almost everyone had a decent enough technical background from reputable colleges, with matching work experience to support their credibility—everyone except for Katrina, our newly appointed general manager. It was absurd and almost laughable when it was Katrina's turn to introduce herself. She flatly stated something similar to this:

"My name is Katrina. I graduated from [a non-technical four years' college]. My major was [biology, which offered no engineering, computer science or any other technical background]. My previous job was [a non-administrative front-end title with no technical background knowledge or requirement] with a great company. Prior to that, I was a substitute biology teacher at [some high school]." As if to make sure no one dared to laugh or question her authority, Katrina quickly scanned the room with a stern look before closing with a "Thank you."

It was a known fact that Katrina had no technical background whatsoever, but Evelyn didn't know that. Everyone could vividly see the surprising look almost jumping out of Evelyn's face as if to say, "How did you get here? How did you get to be the manager of this department, let alone promoted to the general manager of the entire multi-million-dollar company?" But Evelyn was also smart enough to quickly dissipate that look in her face with a smile as Katrina again raised her head to scan the room one more time after her not-so-impressive introduction. And yes, Katrina was looking down at her table almost the entire time she was addressing her team, as if she were hiding something, or as if she were feeling guilty about something she did. Maybe she knew she didn't qualify to lead this team. If she were indeed hiding something else, only she would know. What was frightening to everyone was what she couldn't hide, the fact that she didn't have what one would call the "it" element to lead a team of that caliber.

What kind of connection would she possibly have that would give her the kind of unparalleled privilege one could only dream about? No one knew, and no one dared to ask any questions.

Meanwhile, poor Evelyn looked exasperated and almost flabbergasted, as if she had seen a ghost, to the point where her fake smile seized to work altogether. That was just her first day of work. It went without saying, that no one dared question Katrina openly—that is, if one planned on keeping his or her job. I was just relieved, and thankful to God that Evelyn got to keep hers before she even got the chance to start it.

CHAPTER 8

The First Call of Duty

When My Department Manager Made a Case Against Me

I f working with a clueless leader is an art, then guiding a figuratively blind leader must be a marvel and an embodiment of a completely different persona altogether, for the sake of survival and self-preservation. But, that was exactly what the team did for Katrina. We successfully and anonymously carried her on our collective shoulders from behind the curtain, unappreciated. Maybe it was by design; after all, we were hired and paid to do our jobs. Either way, Katrina still took credit for our achievements, and that was OK. What wasn't OK was the constant and continuous pressure to over-perform that was slowly affecting the morale of the group, especially when the group felt unappreciated and undervalued most of the time.

Team members were clandestinely looking for their exit strategies. Those who were brave enough to voice their opinions on any hot topic regarding any specific project, in any non-submissive manner per Katrina's definition, were let go, sometimes on the spot. They were also only let go within a reasonable time frame, provided their replacement wasn't too hard to find. That was how

I lost two of my friends and favorite colleagues, Joe and Ben, both with whom I was hired the same day.

Katrina fired Joe for being too emotional over a failed project Joe successfully predicted as a result of Katrina's radical leadership. While it was highly unorthodox for a team member to predict his own team's failure; it wasn't that Joe didn't suggest a better solution to the problem at the time. Katrina rejected his approaches. But when it all crumbled down in failure just as Joe openly foretold, she first fired him, then she labeled him loud and full of anger. Ben just couldn't handle it anymore and left on his own. He felt Katrina lied about promoting him from a report analyst role to a software development role. The truth was Katrina simply could not afford to move Ben to any other post at the time; he was just too valuable and was needed as a report analyst, and there was no one to fill his void. Katrina, on the other hand, didn't know how to handle that situation, and things got out of hand. Suddenly, the once steady workplace didn't appear so stable after all, especially when the team was beginning to feel the pressure imploding from within. Maybe new leadership was in order, and just maybe Evelyn's arrival would shine a much-needed outside perspective on things. If history was an indication, it was just a matter of time before Evelyn discovered for herself what she had gotten herself into.

But Evelyn took the job, and it seemed her grace period had ended. While everyone was still excessively nice to her, it did not take a genius to see. Soon Evelyn's core nucleus would be exposed, and everyone would see what she was truly about. The clash was foreseeably imminent. I knew it, the team knew it and she would have to be dumb not to have known it. I didn't know what Evelyn's reaction would be when she finally figured out that the spotless company and perfect manager she was presented at the job interview was anything but.

During Evelyn's first week alone she received visitors from just about every single department. They were as numerable on any given day as people passing before her office door. This was not usual. Someone must have finally told her by the end of the week it was best to keep her office door closed, which she later did to help with the distraction. Just as expected, both Sally and Katrina combined and fed Evelyn as much information as possible about how to do her job, whom to reach out to, whom to befriend and not to befriend and who besides themselves were the major players in the company. The only thing they probably forgot to tell her was who they both really were; no, they could not have done that, as it would have been too revealing. It was, however, something Evelyn would have to discover on her own. Yet they didn't forget to feed Evelyn as much polluted information about me as they could possibly find. Although they didn't have anything spectacularly bad to say about me, they nevertheless sabotaged me to her from the very beginning, and in doing so put an invisible filter between Evelyn and me by which to forever judge me. They painted me to be a bad guy, but I didn't care.

I was only paid to be there and to do work, and not to provide personal enjoyment to anyone, though it would help if we didn't kill each other. All I could do was try my best to stay out any trouble, and more importantly stay alive at the end of each day. The more I thought about it, the more I realized that the only concrete thing both Sally and Katrina had against me was my disagreement with them on certain key issues. That was it. What I struggled to understand was, since when had disagreeing with a colleague over a common issue, while proposing an actual plausible solution, become a crime? Still, that was the reason why they built a case against me. Katrina and Sally gathered selected and otherwise harmless email correspondence between me and them and used it against me. I thought it had to be joke, but it turned out to be anything but.

That was how I became Evelyn's official case, her first call of duty. The assignment both Sally and Katrina gave her was to figure a way to legally punish me for responding in the manner

I had. Sally had already cataloged everything she thought would hurt me and passed it along to Katrina, who in turn added her own input before handing it down to Evelyn. But just in case information in the emails wasn't clear enough, Sally personally highlighted key words she thought were offensive to her even though I had never, not once, used a swear word to address her. My logical reasoning at debunking their flaws was what had made me the enemy; it was what had gotten me in hot water. Katrina would have fired me if she could have afforded it. She had fired other colleagues in the past for wrongdoings far less than the one I was accused of committing. The only problem was, she would have needed to hire a technically savvy professional with a good computer programming background and trained them on our particular software systems for at least six months before she could even begin that process. Also, I was in charge of over 300 individual contractors with whom I had developed personal working relationships. Needless to say, that too didn't make things any easier for her. What Katrina really wanted was to figure out a way to effectively silence me and control me—putting me on a physical dog leash with a cloth stuffed in my mouth would have been her ideal solution. But, since she could not exactly to do that, her next logical step was to send me a strong message. It was unfortunate Evelyn had to be the one to deliver Katrina's blows. I understood who Katrina was and how she operated then, and I didn't hold anything against any of them. I just felt very sorry for Evelyn for being placed in that tough position.

I had met with Evelyn. She was a nice and wonderful young lady full of life, who enjoyed the outdoors. She had told me so herself during our scheduled one-on-one meeting; the one she was required to hold with everyone in our technical team, now her team. She was also very smart, thoughtful and funny. I overheard she had created an online company when she was just in her early 20s. I didn't ask her anything about that; she did not bring it up to me. Our first meeting was more a getting-to-know-you meeting. We let our guards down in a relaxed setting, her new office, and just talked for a few minutes about random things. She asked about my son, who was then just a few months old. "He's good," I responded without adding any additional detail. I have long decided to keep my family life as far away from my work life as I possibly could; and this meant keeping my family out of any topic of discussion.

Evelyn didn't have any children of her own then, but she had a boyfriend, and she liked to run. I asked her what her time was on her first marathon. "About three-and-a-half hours," she replied, which I just knew could not be true. Being a runner myself, I just couldn't bring myself to accept that number from her. I had just met her, but I could tell she couldn't be that fast; in fact, I thought I was in better physical shape than she was. I have been an athlete my entire life, and I wasn't that fast for that time; she would have been running an average pace of about six to seven minutes a mile. Four to five hours would have been her correct answer, but who was I to call her on a lie? As far as I was concerned, I wouldn't have objected even if she told me she was an actual angel and could literally fly. After all, she could have been an angel for being in a position to even attempt to fix our current office situation for all I knew.

I had also seen Evelyn walking and getting too cozy with David, my coworker who happened to be an attractive young man of about the same age as her, as if they were a couple. Maybe she was trying to fix him too, or was it the other way around? Didn't Evelyn say she had a boyfriend? The whole thing was confusing to me. Either way, I thought I liked her, and she was nice to me. Evelyn, unlike her manager Katrina, and Sally, had no negative energy around her. Her aura was clear and almost pearl white with pleasant colors on the edges. It was apparent Evelyn came in peace and meant well. I could also tell she was neither judgmental nor sarcastic—again, unlike her manager. She was rather warm, was full of excitement and actually seemed to be listening while we were talking. Evelyn also didn't talk over me or cut me off right in the middle of my sentences because I was taking my time to carefully communicate my ideas.

Evelyn heard I was into distance running as well. That must have come out during our team introduction; or was it David who told her? I have run with him twice in the past, and he seemed to have avoided my running mate and I ever since. Both times, David challenged us to five-kilometer runs, and my running mate destroyed him both times. I have declined the challenge both times, but ran the course at my own pace anyway. I was nevertheless glad my running mate severely beat him by well over a mile. In fact, I had done numerous five-kilometer (5K) races and a dozen or so 10Ks, and a couple of half marathons, but never a full marathon—at least not yet. And I wasn't looking to run any of them with David, not anytime soon.

On the day when Katrina decided to punish me for daring to have a disagreement with her and Sally, she had first gone through all the disciplinary procedures in the company's Human Resources (HR) handbook to determine what punishment would best fit my crime. When she couldn't find anything that satisfied her desire, she felt compelled to settle for whatever she was lawfully able to pin on me for offense. In fact, my transgression that warranted the upmost degree of punishment was handwritten and circled on the tightly stapled documents Katrina had Evelyn serve me. It simply read: "Communication." It was preposterous they had to make up my transgression, because it wasn't in the employee handbook. Not knowing what was going on, I was first surprised by the sight of Katrina in the room. This was supposed to be my regular one-on-one scheduled meeting with Evelyn and the second one since she took office.

"Hey Dee," said Evelyn with a smile.

"Hi," I responded directly, looking at both of them, her and Katrina. I was dressed in a Kathy pan and a white, short-sleeve polo shirt. I didn't feel the need to wear my reading glasses that

I only wear when I am in front of my computer. Some have said they make me look very smart, but I didn't think I needed them. *What was going on here? Could this be a trap?* I couldn't help but think to myself. Looking at them both together, I knew right away nothing good could possibly come out of this meeting. Katrina has been circling me like a hungry shark for about a month or so now. She must have found on me a weak spot and decided to move in for the kill. I quickly reviewed in my head possible reasons why these two would want to corner me. *Have I done anything wrong recently? No!* But if I did, I must not have been aware of it. *Have I knowingly stepped on someone's toes? No!* Again, if I did that it was a complete accident. I could not recall anything I had done that would have been so outrageous that it warranted those two cornering me in a room. Right at that moment, my guards were up, my senses were heightened, and with Katrina in that room I was prepared for the worst. I also had to slow down my heartbeat and my racing mind just to be able to hear myself think.

"Please have a seat," I thought I heard someone say to me. I saw Evelyn's mouth move. That must have been her. I slowly sat down in the spare chair in her office, almost facing the entrance door that was now closed behind me.

"Hum, I don't know of an easier way to put this for you, but we have decided on a disciplinary action against you; I am sorry," said Evelyn quietly with Katrina directly looking at her as if to make sure Evelyn was saying exactly what she has been coached to say.

"Disciplinary action?' I was almost surprised and released at the same time, for I was expecting the worst; at least that explained Katrina's presence. And then I quickly caught myself. "What disciplinary action? What have I done?"

With that, Evelyn handed me a stack of papers stapled together listing my gravest offenses. I was amused and almost laughed at first. Although I had some idea about what they were trying to get me for, I was actually eager to read the document, as I was sure Katrina and Sally had their hands in it. Why wouldn't they? They both hated me and wanted to kill me; Katrina said so herself. As far as I was concerned, seeing me punished would have been a bad day in the office for them. My question, then, that I didn't bother to ask was: *Why did Katrina have to put poor Evelyn in the middle of this?* She just started working, and already they felt the need to make her the bad cop in my eyes—not that I actually labeled her that way. How evil of Katrina. What a way to spook the poor lady.

I quickly glanced over the document before flipping through the pages. The document had my name nicely written on the top of it; at least they got that one right. It also had the words "Disciplinary Action" somewhere on that same front page; great, now we are talking. I sarcastically muttered something out with a smile, which even I couldn't recall til this day. This caused both Katrina and Evelyn to look at each other confusedly. I was trying to make sense of something, everything, and thinking about how I could have actually defended myself. That was almost impossible. If anything, I should have thanked Katrina for not firing me, or literally firing at me since she hated me so much and wanted to kill me. Instead of being predictably upset, I felt amused and grateful, and I really wanted to thank them both; but at the same time I resisted the urges, for that could have come across wrong or sarcastic.

On one page was a list of available offenses to pick from with a check box next to each for anyone to check. They included: "Poor Performance, Tardiness, Theft of Company Property, Insubordination, Fighting at Work, Weapon at Work," etc. Mine had to be handwritten: "communication," it said, circled in black. Since when had communicating or conveying one's ideas, where ideas were supposed to be welcomed, become a crime? I couldn't help but think to myself while flipping through the pages. Then it hit me. This wasn't about my communication issue at all. Many things were running through my mind, but protesting the document or the punishment wouldn't have been the wisest thing to do.

My reaction to their corrective action would have been what Katrina wanted. That would have been her perfect excuse to bring an even heavier hammer down on me. I couldn't have possibly gone down like that; I was way too smart for her. I would not have minded getting fired, but damaging my good name really concerned me. That was the only thing I could not afford to do. So I decided to humble myself and accept whatever punishment they had in mind. I decided to calmly but objectively play the hand I was dealt. If I was lucky, maybe this would be nothing but a joke—a joke I could look back on sometime in the distant future and laugh. What I needed then was some time to think and to make a decision about what to do next. After all, I was a family man with a fiancée and a baby; and I needed to make a decision that was not in my best interest but in their best interest. And right then, keeping my job was in the best interest of my family.

The entire document was but printed copies of past emails, some as old as two years old. I had sent Sally emails to explain certain project solutions on which we had a disagreement. Sally made sure to highlight in yellow key words and sometime entire segments she thought were offensive to her. One of them almost made me laugh; it read, "Please let me know if you need further detailed explanation to understand this process." That was my writing. I wrote that line because I provided explanation to a question regarding a particular issue and was hoping to elaborate on it if need be, and now they were taking it out of context and using it against me? This was pathetic to say the least.

There was also an email exchange with Katrina about a day off we talked about earlier, and that she had failed to approve. So now, I'm trying to understand why someone told me she would do something in person on two separate occasions, and then later refused to do it. Is that a crime? Katrina added her own note in ink that read: "Dee took the pleasure to take an unapproved day off and then showed up to work unexpectedly." She was referring to the Monday after the Thanksgiving holiday, when I came to work after I realized she approved neither the Friday nor the Monday after Thanksgiving I had requested a few months ahead of time. I didn't have any defense for any of her charges; I should have known better to never trust her.

I was almost surprised when I saw the last page. It was a printout of an email, a response to one of Cherise's many open emails to everyone in the office regarding an old project. In that email, I dared to tell Cherise that we (the collective we working on the project helping the client) could have done a better job as a team informing contractors when they committed certain preventable mistakes the first time around. I even explained my reasoning by also stating that it would help mitigate the likelihood of contractors repeating the same mistakes. It was so ridiculous Katrina and her friends felt the need to degrade themselves to that level. Cherise, a colleague from the project approval department, was apparently upset at me. But not for reasons you might suspect. Cherise was mad at me for including everyone on that email, when all I was actually doing was replying to the same email she had initially sent, carbon-copying (cc'ing) the same group of recipients on it. *What is wrong with these people?* I couldn't help but think to myself. Cherise too obviously hated me for contradicting her and for apparently correcting her in an open email, while all I was doing was offering my idea on a particular matter she had raised. *Are these people OK? Could this get any weirder? Again, what is wrong with these people, or better yet, what kind of culture are these people trying to promote?* Those were my exact thoughts; I didn't dare to voice them. I suddenly raised my head, only to meet both Katrina's and Evelyn's eyes looking directly back at me.

I could almost feel Evelyn's pain as her facial expression rapidly switched from innocent and playful to serious. *Poor Evelyn, why did they do this to you?* I thought to myself. Katrina's facial expression didn't budge, as she was out for blood from the get go. It remained as stern as it was when I first came through the door. Katrina didn't need to pretend to like me; she knew I knew how she felt about me, and that was okay by me. The truth also was, she knew I knew her better than Evelyn. I stared at them both for a few long seconds, hoping either one of them would break the silence and say something unexpectedly. Either way, I wanted to sense if there was something else going on that they were not telling me at that very moment. Then I heard Katrina softly clearing her throat. *She couldn't be getting ready to spit in my face, could she?*

"Hum, hum you know …" she said, "we are here to help if you want to talk about anything."

Great, now she wants to talk, I heard my mind speaking again. *But, about what? Who does she think I am? Do I look like an idiot now? Did she really think that if I wanted to talk, I would come to her?*

I again plunged my eyes back into the document without saying a word to her or Evelyn, as if to tell Katrina, "Please give me a minute to digest this information." Then I saw something I thought could help: the company's HR information. The document explicitly said to call HR at the number provided for details and additional information. It also briefly stated what my sentence was: "Three hours of communication counseling fully paid for by the company." That was comforting.

"Thank you," I sincerely said to both Sally and Katrina while looking directly into their eyes. Then pointing to this document, I added, "I think I need some time to digest this one first." On that tune, I got up and exited the room. A sudden silence fell over them and the entire place. It was so quiet; one could actually hear a pin drop.

I went home that day wondering if I could have handled things a little differently. Yes, I could have. I should not have played into Sally's hands by responding to her provocative emails; it was a trap and I should have known better. Lesson learned! That was my only and biggest regret. I did not regret responding to Cherise, because she knew I was right. I wasn't trying to shut her off even though she deserved to be shut off at the time; that wasn't my cup of tea. I was nevertheless happy. My comment shined some light on her. I didn't mind if it got into trouble much later. Katrina, well, she needed not to be answered. It was just a matter of time before she fell off her pedestal—her undeserved, white high-horse management job title she thought was synonymous to abuse. I was certain if everything worked out for me according to plan; I would not even be there to witness her fall. I wouldn't even have anything to do with that. That was already her own doing, since she was causing all the best talents around her to flee one at a time. The funny thing about wicked intent was it would always find a way to bubble to the surface regardless of the depth at which it was buried. That was just how things naturally work. The same was true for lies and deceptions, and those practicing them.

My heart really went out to Evelyn, who I was certain had passed on other opportunities to get the role of local manager. She had just landed and already was beginning to question her decision. Could she have done better at a different company? Absolutely, yes! I wished her the very best, as I sincerely hoped she survived that workplace. As for me and my talent, we didn't want to stay there another minute. But for the sake of my family, I decided to play it safe and linger just long enough until the time was right, until I found myself a better home. I have since become self-conscious and distrusting of my surroundings as a result of that incident, especially of power hungry and bullying colleagues and authorities alike.

I was grateful to have survived that incident, as I knew deep down there was a hidden meaning behind it all. What could the possible underlying message or messages be? That was a quest for another day. But I knew I was getting free counseling out of it. As far as I was concerned, that was cause for a celebration. I was definitely sure I would get an opportunity to learn something good out of that. I was a winner in this ordeal after all, as that was my wakeup call. And it was loud and clear. I too would start looking for an exit strategy and would have the opportunity to make that move on my own terms. All of the sudden the light bulbs just went off; it became clear to me. I needed to reevaluate my career path and objectives and take some necessary but corrective actions. I planned on taking some online courses to help work on my problem area to better my chances while positioning myself for the leap ahead.

After this, the HR department had Evelyn schedule a mandatory meeting for Sally and me in their attempt to sort out our communication issues, as it was known, for which Evelyn was the mediator. Sally was the bad apple and the root cause of the issue. When she showed up to the meeting with a list of paper works to instruct me on how to communicate with her, I in return slipped to Evelyn a printed, saved email I'd never sent to anyone, in which I detailed to Evelyn what I knew Sally was trying to accomplish. I explicitly stated the sole purpose of Sally putting me through this shenanigan was her attempt to make me look bad and get me in some kind of trouble.

I neither exposed Sally for being the sorceress she was, nor addressed her in any disrespectful manner. Yet she got so upset, got up and nearly stormed out of the room because I dared slip a note to Evelyn without first consulting her or sharing the same information with her. Evelyn had to quickly stop her, and so prevented her from dramatizing an already tense situation. What I did do was completely stop exchanging emails with Sally no matter how innocent or provocative they were. I have chosen to copy or involve a third party on every single one of our important interactions, whether it was a one-on-one meeting or important job-related emails, and have also avoided being alone with Sally at all costs. That was something Sally desperately wanted; allowing her that opportunity would have been a very regrettable mistake. Sally nearly lost her job that day, and had she walked out of that meeting like she intended to do, she would have. I was glad she didn't, because then she would be more than happy to sing to everyone that I was the reason why she got fired, or had any disciplinary action taken against her. I have determined not to have anything to do with her.

"Only with your eyes shall you behold and see the
reward of the wicked."
—Psalms 91:8 (King James Version)

The tone of the meeting changed for the worse the very minute Sally jumped out of her seat, and no matter how hard Evelyn tried to bring it back on course, her efforts were not very productive. The meeting ended on a dry note, with both Evelyn and I having to write a detailed report to the HR department about how it went.

After that meeting, and after I have talked to the HR department, I called and scheduled my first appointment with a counseling office; I enjoyably began to serve my time for the crime deemed to have been committed. I could not have been any happier for the opportunity to meet with Doctor Bob Meetos, my counselor and a great therapist who helped me see the light at the end of my tunnel. Believe it or not, I was grateful for everything that transpired up til that point, because it paved the way to all the promising things that were to come.

That incident must have traumatized Evelyn as well, because she handed in her resignation letter less than three months after that occurrence. This was just a week after two distinct colleagues, a software developer and a report analyst, voluntarily resigned. Evelyn also must have figured out she could have done better elsewhere. Evelyn accepted a job offer with a different company just to get away from it all. Two weeks later, I too followed suit for a chance at a new beginning somewhere where I, my talents and my contributions would hopefully be appreciated.

CHAPTER 9

Guilty

Serving the Sentence

I enjoyably began serving time for the crime that the others deemed I had committed, at a counseling facility not far from the company site. The scheduled hour-long meeting with a professional communication counselor by the name of Doctor Robert Meetos (Bob) was probably what I needed to work on my communication skills. I also sought help with anything else he could assist me with. I figured there was only so much we could fit into three-hour-long sessions, but I remained open to the idea. Whatever I could learn would hopefully serve as a tool that could benefit me in the future.

In the end, however, the punishment didn't seem like a punishment after all. I found the sessions gave me an opportunity to learn and to reeducate myself, and in doing so, to become a better person. That felt good, a true blessing in disguise, maybe. The way I saw it, Katrina might have intended to inflict a punishment on me, but God in his wisdom turned it into a blessing. She and her friends had found me guilty of a crime I did not feel was a crime at all, but they had been limited in the punishment they could decide for me. That had been up to the company's HR. was that luck, or was it God's grace?

I went to my first appointment and met with Doctor Meetos, who insisted I called him Bob. Bob was a wonderful guy with a larger-than-life personality. He was a big man, weighing easily 300-plus pounds, and he was strong. He could have been a football player, a linebacker. Bob was a black, physically imposing man with a strong presence and a deep voice. I didn't inquire as to whether he had been an athlete when he was younger. It didn't seem appropriate. In any case, my company had paid him to make me the topic of our discussion at least for the length of the three sessions.

Bob's office was along one of Schenectady's main boulevards. Thanks to my Global Position System (GPS), a modern-day personal digital map, a device that could literally direct anyone to an otherwise unknown destination, I made it to my appointment safely and on time.

I didn't need to know the place in advance; I just needed to know the address, which Bob gave me over the phone. Once I entered that coordinate into the device, the rest was history. It was that simple. Getting to my destination was just a matter of following the directions given by a live map moving at the pace of my moving vehicle, and talking.

Yes, the digital map was talking to me as if it were a live, talking companion in the car with me. Between the interrupted "Turn left," "Turn right," "Prepare for a left or right turn ahead," "Make a U-turn when it is safe," and "Recalculating" in case you made the wrong turn, the GPS device is a great and wonderful invention.

It has single-handedly taken the planning out of road trips, and in doing so has also saved a ton of time. Preparations that originally went into mapping trips to try and prevent travelers the agony of potentially getting lost and having to ask complete strangers for directions, are now rare occurrences. Of course, GPS isn't exactly perfect. Some travelers have been found stranded on roads less traveled, or in some cases were directed to drive across a body of water like a lake or a river, or in some cases into plantation fields. Funny stories have surfaced about of how GPS has led drivers to strange places, and have found their ways to the evening news of both local and national media. Thankfully, I made it to the appointment on time.

Beside the 30-minute drive from work to Doctor Bob Meetos' office, and another half-hour drive I would be making later after the session, I thought it was a great investment for which I didn't even need to pay, except with my time, but I wouldn't really call that a payment—rather, it was a small contribution into my personal growth. The only thing not so great about it was that it ended up making my days continuous and longer than usual. Again, that was a very small price for the hopefully invaluable knowledge I would be gaining from the sessions.

Bob's office looked like a regular house partitioned into small occupational rooms, which I likened to small offices. Bob didn't have a receptionist from what I was able to see; aluminum wind charms strategically placed behind the entrance door sufficed. The reception area wasn't spacious either. It was just big enough to sit four people comfortably across from each other with a small coffee table between them. In the right angle of the roof, directly facing the chairs, hung a small flat-screen television from the wall. The TV was completely muted but captioned in English; written words displayed and scrolled from left to right. They seemed to be moving as fast as the newsman or anyone else spoke on the TV for that matter. The only time it didn't scrawl much was when there was music playing, or some other type of noise like some explosion or something. I guessed it was because the TV wasn't exactly sure how to interpret some of the noises; but it did automatically resume captioning as soon as any meaningful words were being spoken.

That too was amazing. I lost track of the news after my eyes gave up reading so quickly at the speed of the spoken words. They wandered around the room as I waited for Bob, who only came out to let his clients in one at the time on their exact appointed time. I was beginning to wonder, what would happen if someone failed to show up exactly on time? Would Bob wait for them, or carry on? I guessed he would probably call to check on their whereabouts and then carry on if they couldn't make it in within a reasonable timeframe. I wouldn't want to be kept waiting there forever, I thought. Bob came out from the small hallway to greet and accompany a lady into his office; I guessed she was a client who came in before me. However, their meeting was unusually brief and lasted less than 20 minutes; I thought that was odd. Maybe she only needed 20-minute therapy.

Then it occurred to me: Bob must be running the entire office by himself. He was a lone wolf. If this was the case, he must have either been new in the business or just didn't have a big client base. My eyes wandered around the room some more as I waited. In the far left-hand side of the room was a movable plastic jug water fountain; and directly across from it were coat hangers with no coats hanging on them. On the coffee table was a stack of health and sport magazines and only a single local newspaper. There also was a small ball full of red and white hard-minted candies. I was not a big fan of candies, so I picked up one of the sport magazines to read. On the cover was a picture of the athlete of the day—who else but LeBron James, a famous basketball player who had routinely been in the news lately for various reasons. Born and raised in Akron, Ohio. Mr. James found his way to stardom on the basketball court where he had dominated since childhood. Mr. James has pretty much dominated the sport with his pure strength and high basketball IQ. While he has failed on a couple of occasions to win a National Basketball Association (NBA) title for his beloved home fans of Cleveland, Ohio, Mr. James didn't fail to do the same thing twice with a different

NBA team in Miami, Florida. He is both loved and hated by basketball fans all over the world because, believe it or not, Mr. James made a return to his home state in his quest to win his home state fans a title, and to break what was wildly know as a "championship drought curse" hanging over the state—another sport superstition. Though fascinating, I was beginning to find the News repetitive and already annoying. If only I could change the channel.

Just then, Bob came through the small corridor:

"Good morning, Dee. Did I say your name right, or you wouldn't mind me calling you by your first name?"

"Please call me Dee"

"Come with me then, Dee," Bob effortlessly said, and turned around. I could almost see the shadow of the lady that went in the room before me exiting the office. She was still holding her jacket in her arm. I quickly looked right before me to my left then to my right so as to have a better sense of my surroundings. I had been right: The office wasn't that big, and there was no other room at the end of the corridor.

Bob opened the office door on the right-hand side.

"Please have a seat, Dee, and make yourself comfortable," Bob said, pointing to the nice and very comfortable-looking black sofa in the center of the room.

"Thank you," I responded, quickly glancing over the room with my eyes wide open, and waiting for him to sit before I sat down. On second thought, I went ahead and sat down; he had told me so himself, hadn't he? It was a nice and relaxing room with a big window to the outside. There were a few books neatly displayed in the bookshelves in front of me and on the coffee table behind me. There was no table between the sofa where I was sitting and the leather armchair directly facing me where Bob was sitting. There was complete silence for a moment. This room must have been meticulously designed with comfort and ease in mind, I thought. But then it was a therapy room.

"How are you, Dee?" said Bod in his deep and overwhelming voice.

"Good, thank you for asking. I feel comfortable already," I told Bob with a big smile, knowing too well that was the aim of the room's setting.

"Oh, well, thank you," Bob added, and went straight to work. "This is your very first visit, right?"

"Right, this is my first visit"

"I am going to have to get you to do pretty much what I ask of every first-time visitor." He handed me a stack of paperwork. "These will be some of our agreements, and here are a few other documents I am lawfully bound to give you. Please remember to sign the top form so I can get paid. And please don't hesitate to ask me any questions."

I quickly glanced over the paperwork and signed the one he referred to. I didn't read much of the remaining document since I would be taking it home with me anyway.

"So Dee, what brings you in here today?" Bob casually asked as if he wasn't expecting much of any answer in return.

What brought me in that day? Well, Bob looked at me as though he might have been a preacher or a pastor at some point in his life. He had a calm demeanor about him. The tone of his voice, the gaze of his look, the way he dressed and even the pauses, the empty voids between his sentences when he was speaking were almost commanding. He struck me as someone who really knew what he was doing; but that wasn't what brought me in that day. He knew why I was there.

"Well Bob, to be honest with you, this was supposed to be my punishment for daring to speak the truth and my honest opinion at work on certain key issues I thought I was right about."

"What do you mean by that? What happened?"

"Well, I could tell you the story from the very beginning, but that would take up the entire session, so I am going to try to be as brief as possible."

"I am listening …"

"Well, long story short, certain people in my office, but mainly my manager, wanted me silenced. They didn't want my input on hot-topic issues—not that I wanted to provide any. It just so happened that when the issue involved me, I believed I had the right to … I wouldn't say defend myself, but defend my ideas and my reasoning." I paused and looked at him as if to say, are you following me?

"I am listening …"

"I know I could have been a little bit more careful dealing with certain people, but I wasn't. And that was my own wrongdoing. I have no one to blame but myself."

"Tell me about the instance when this occurred."

"There was a time where I felt something was off following a project we worked on. One of my coworkers in particular, I won't mention any name, wanted me to take the fall or the blame for the project."

"I am listening …"

"There wasn't blame. It turned out I had resolved the issue correctly; it just so happened that my methodology wasn't exactly clear to her, so instead of asking me to explain it to her, she went and spread lies about me. She made me look bad," I continued. "While it was a rather bizarre situation, I believe it might have been the tipping point, which might have destroyed our work relationship. This project in question wasn't what I thought was the issue, but rather a mere reason to point fingers at me and sabotage me."

"What do you mean?"

"Well, for starters I overheard my manager telling this coworker of mine—you know, the one who wanted to have me accept blame for a project I properly handled after it had gone through a lot of changes. My manager told her that she hated and wanted to kill me; in her own words. I overheard her saying, 'I hate this kid, and I want to kill him.'"

"Ok!"

"I think this might have inadvertently given that coworker permission to try her own scheme of things on me."

"I see." Bob paused, looked at me for a minute, then resumed.

"What is your religious inclination, if you don't mind me asking?" asked Bob. I was shocked and completely caught off guard by Bob's response, or rather question.

"Pardon me?"

"What do you believe in? Most people believe in something. What do you believe in, if you have any?" Bob said softly, repeatedly looking me square in the face as though his next response depended on my answer.

"Well," I slowly said while still keeping an eye on him just in case he burst into flame at the hearing of my answer. "I am a Christian; I believe in God and Jesus Christ as my personal Lord and savior." Then I waited for him, for something to happen. Bob didn't burst into flame as I was imagining him in my mind. That was good.

"What would Jesus do?"

"Pardon me, what do you mean?"

"I have heard your story. I want to know if it was Jesus in your shoes, what he would have done?" Bob responded, still directly looking into my face.

"Well, when you put it like that, then … what would Jesus do?" I repeated the question back to me just to see how much it weighed. "I believe Jesus would not have retaliated or responded in anger; this is because He was a prince of peace," I said without any hint of hesitation.

Jesus could have done many things because he was human. Though a son of God he still perceived things from a human point of view. I might not have known exactly what he would do, but I had a pretty good idea about what he wouldn't do. Maybe Bob would rebuke my answer; maybe he wouldn't. After all, I didn't know anything about his religious affiliation. People from different backgrounds have different views about Jesus, the savior and son of God. In fact, I wasn't even sure if Bob personally knew or had ever experienced this Jesus he was asking me about. My ears were mostly ready for an explosion, so I pretty much shut them within me. Then he continued.

"Do you know why Jesus would have done that?" To the sound of that, my heartbeat, I was steadily holding slowly returned to normal.

"He would have done that, I am thinking, to avoid confrontation and preserve peace."

"Then why are you eating yourself up as though you have suffered a great mishap?" Now I was totally and completely lost. Did Bob just spin the subject on me?

"I don't think I suffered anything Bob. In fact, I only talked and communicated when I absolutely felt it was necessary. I felt keeping silent would have been worse in my case; it would have meant consenting to them." Then I waited for him to weight in.

"You did well in not starting a fight or an argument."

"Well, that wasn't an option. I could have been fired," I said to Bob with a smile. "I hope you see where I am coming from."

I went on to tell Bob about the email incidents, and the workplace tension that resulted from it. I also told him about how I felt threatened coming to work every day and felt the need to constantly check my back. I didn't tell him that I felt the need to stay vigilant and alert at all times; he already figured that out. I wanted Bob to teach me something I didn't already know. I wanted to learn something beneficial from the sessions that could be applicable to my life and my future. So I asked him.

"You have heard me speak my mind. How can you help me?" Bob seemed almost delighted with me asking that question. His eyes brightened as he leaned forward.

"I am glad you ask," said Bob with excitement. "For starters, you ought to completely stop replying to that coworker of your's emails if you can help it. Take note and wise up. I don't know if you are listening to yourself, but it seems she and everyone else involved are fueled by your own ammunition. Just stop feeding them, and the problem will die away." Bob then paused, as if he were digging deep inside to tell me something that seemed to be eluding him. He closed his eyes and looked down and around. He must have been thinking.

I was fighting the urge to say something. But I just couldn't bring myself to interrupt him. Bob is the professional here, and I the student—or in some weird way, the patient. I needed to let the silence run its normal course. It wasn't my job to break it; it was his. When I thought I was losing this war on silence, Bob said something.

"Hum, hum … I am going to try to relate to you for just a moment here, OK? I think you knew about his biblical character," he said. "Joseph I am sure his name was."

"Yes, the biblical Joseph who became the second in command in Egypt after going through some very difficult circumstances in his personal life?" I asked, hoping I was right, and we were actually talking about the same biblical character.

"Yes, that one. When his bother tossed him into a pit and later sold him as a slave, what did he do? He forgave and moved on. What did God do? He blessed him later as a result."

"OK?" Where Bob was going with this was a question I didn't need answered.

"The point here is, it is not what happened to you that define who you are. It is your attitude and what you do from there forward that will shape you? Do you follow me?"

"Yes, I do"

"Ok, good" He quickly checked his wrist and saw the time. His eyes widened. "Ok, ok, I think we might be running out of time here. Let's wrap up today's session. Next time, I don't want to hear anything about that manager or your coworker of yours trying to hurt you. OK? That will not help you a bit. Let's talk about how to you turn the table around and use this moment to your advantage.

Do you hear me?" he added authoritatively, as if he were talking to a friend or someone he really cared about, while maintaining a direct eye contact with me.

"OK."

"Great! Let's make the best of this situation now," he said it in a semi-funny voice while arranging some of the paperwork he was holding in his hands. "When can we meet next?"

"Next week. Would the same day and time work for you?" I suggested.

"Good, see you next week, the same day and time," Bob repeated while shaking my hand and getting ready to walk me to the door.

I have never knowingly talked to a psychologist or any professional of his kind of profession before in my entire life, with the exception of my college counselor, I must admit. He made a lot of sense. Everything became clear to me from that very moment. I think I knew what to do next; I was going to be focusing on how to use this experience to help me grow and become a better person. I was going to play it safe at work until I was ready to move.

I felt great meeting with Bob; I couldn't even begin to explain how I felt deep down inside. I honestly felt transformed. In just less than one hour of conversation, Bob had successfully helped me unlock hidden things and opened my mind to see things I could have seen myself but hadn't. Already, I couldn't wait for our next session.

CHAPTER 10

The Flying Snake

Staying Defiant Even When Things Are Dreadfully Difficult

I had run the day before. Long and steady runs were as good for my heart as they were for my mind, body and soul. They helped stabilize my thought process and have done a great job at keeping me in sync, well-balanced, sane and at peace with myself and my surroundings. Running allows me time to isolate myself and just think. This is how I have come to think about things in a more natural yet direct way, on my feet and engaged: the sound of my heartbeat, concentrating on my inhalations as well as my exhalations, the calling of the birds in their natural environment, and of course the modern-day commotions of people always rushing to a destination of some sort, the passing cars, airplanes flying above and the noises of a distant locomotive. That was where I mostly felt more alive, fearless and defiant. I would not back down to anything, no to this, and definitely not to that, or the one which was yet to come.

The weather was turning cold. I could feel it as the Saturday morning breeze melted against my steamy face. I knew it wasn't too cold for a jacket; I had my long-sleeve, light-weight running fleece on. Overall, I had a good and invigorating run that day. I came home to a warm shower and felt ready for life and whatever else the world might have in store for me. I felt the same way I felt after every single one of my runs: recharged and ready to go.

A couple of days later, I had the same fleece with me, only this time I was at work. I wasn't wearing it. I had long taken it off and hung it on the back of my chair, as I often did before facing my workstation, composed of a computer desk located in the corner of the middle cubicle where my docked laptop, connected to two medium-sized monitors that have been waiting for me ever since I started working with the company. Winter was definitely inching in on us, but that wasn't what was making me feel cold inside. Something seemed out of place, and although I could feel it in my bones, I didn't really know what it was. I wasn't able to put my finger on it, and that bothered me greatly.

My senses were triggered the very minute I sat down that morning, sending a chilling feeling down my spine that stuck with me for several hours. Oh, and yes, I could feel things. In fact, I could sense things you would not believe. Spending every single day of my working moment looking over my shoulders, observing and analyzing my environment constantly, had forced me to subconsciously activate inner senses I didn't even know I had. This had been going on for a few months now.

The office heating system seemed to be fully functioning that day, explaining why nobody actually complained about the cold all day. If something was wrong with it, I certainly did not know, and someone would have said something already. The occasional "Wow, it is too cold in here," or "Can someone please lower the heat, we are not bacon in an oven, you know," were often good indicators. I certainly would not be the first to raise my voice about the heating system; that just wasn't how I went about things in that office. I had tried to keep as low a profile as I possibly could. My ultimate hope was to do my job well, and most importantly to avoid stepping on anyone's toes—to stay out of trouble. So I have learned staying invisible helped in that area. What I did not know then was that trouble was all around me the whole time in the person of Sally, and she had been especially trying to find any weakness in my defensive system. Although I wasn't sick that day, I really felt as though I was maybe because of the unexplainable feeling of suspense in the air. It felt as if something was ready to happen. Still, I was about my business as usual; I was at work, after all.

I did my usual routine: I checked my to-do list first thing that morning and prioritized my tasks. I knew exactly what to do first, whom to contact about the prior day's transactions, and what task to close right away. The ones that were not initially important I carefully pushed down the list. I answered a few calls and addressed some issues over the phone. I also replied to a lot of project-specific emails to clients and closed a few projects in the process. I was in my normal work zone until the ringing of a phone caught my attention.

It was in the cubicle adjacent to mine; the call came in on Sally's personal cell phone. When you have worked alongside someone for over three and a half years, if you are even remotely anywhere in the neighborhood of being smart, you tend to pick up on their habits, and a few other things. You also learn to know if and when something is out of place. I was able to tell the difference between certain things. For instance, that phone call was unlike any other countless calls I have heard Sally answer in the past; this was different. She quickly grabbed the phone and started to run down the hallway, passing Evelyn's office, on her way outside before even answering the call. That was the first time I have seen her literally run. That was no ordinary call; that was a call she had been expecting. And something tells me it was probably about me. Ever since, Sally realized she couldn't harm me with her dark magic; she had been looking for help to do it in other ways. I felt it in my gut; I just knew. While I did not know who made the call or what the specific exchange was, I knew my name was somehow mentioned. This wasn't just because Sally never behaved that way before the entire time I knew her; it was also her demeanor before and after the call. She was very suspicious, to say the least, looking at me from the corner of one eye and doing her toe walk again.

I needed to get back to work, so I quickly brushed off that thought and covered my ears with a pair of headphones. Whenever I could, I played an audio Bible on my computer from the Internet; this was my escape gateway. The live scripture helped me not only get away from my day-to-day problems, but it also allowed me the opportunity to learn more about my God and his plan and purpose for my life. As I marveled at the comforting messages, I couldn't help but hear some of my uppermost questions answered as the audio played on. So I kept listening.

Coming back to reality, I had a strange feeling that something was happening. I could actually sense a storm was coming. Although I didn't know what kind of storm it was or where it was coming from, I was not afraid—not at all. What I did know was the simple fact that God was in my corner, and he promised to never let me down or forsake me. I also knew he would level the playing field and turn my shortcomings into triumphant moments. God the father was my defender after all; whom shall I fear? None, nobody! Thanks to our Lord and savior Jesus Christ, who took my sins and the world's to the cross with him, and was raised from the dead spotless. Through him I was forever viewed in the eyes of the Father, I am now a new creation in him, my savior. Whom then shall I fear? What can mere mortals do to me?

I came home from work that day feeling extremely uneasy, though I knew I shouldn't. I did not recognize what it was. And while I really wanted to share my emotion with someone, I did not know whom to trust or turn to with that kind of information. I would have loved to speak to my brother Emanuel, but he was unfortunately an ocean away, somewhere in Africa. I kneeled down for just a few minutes to meditate and said a simple prayer, like I always did before I went to work, while I was on my way to work, before I sat down to begin my day, while my day was unfolding, before I got out of work, while I was in my car home from work, before I got out of my car to go home, while I entered home, before I had my dinner, after I had my dinner and before I went to bed for the day.

Heavenly Lord
I thank you for this moment you have given me,
for your presence in my life,
for protecting and watching over me,
for being my God and savior, and
for guiding my every step, my every move.
Glory, Blessings and Hallelujah to your Holy Name
in Jesus Christ's name. Amen

My entire life was about short, little prayers and staying in constant communication with God the Father. This was a habit which I chose to form a long time ago, when I was just about 10 years of age. It was, in fact, a secret, one I accidentally picked up from one of my favorite aunts from my mother's side. Aunt Tamar was just a few years older than I was since she was the youngest, the baby of five children my grandparents had birthed. Growing up with three elder sisters and a brother has both its ups and downs. Aunt Elisabeth was the first born, my mother Jacqueline was the second, followed by aunt Messy the third; Uncle Jim was the fourth child and came before aunt Tamar. Aunty Tamar wasn't really picked on as the youngest growing up, but they didn't let her get away with anything, either. She was always hard-working, trying to please pretty much everyone. After all, she was the baby and approvals were that much more important to her. Not me. Unlike Aunty Tamar, who knew she was the baby and often sought everyone's approval, I didn't even know I was growing up with my grandparents, and called them mom and pop and actually thought they were my biological parents. I was confused often, so

I often rolled with the punches and weighed my actions carefully against my good judgment, hoping they were safe enough to pass without further approval. If they weren't, I often quickly found out and didn't repeat them.

On that day, Aunty Tamar was having a casual conversation with Tiffany, one of her childhood friends, when I got interested and quietly eavesdropped into their conversation.

"You know," Tamar told her friend Tiffany, "you probably would not believe me on this, but I have discovered a secret that has literally transformed my life."

"What would that be?" Tiffany asked.

"What I am about to tell you is an honest truth, and I guarantee you. In fact, I more than guarantee you; I would even put my life on it if it would help you believe me that staying in constant communication with God works like magic." Aunt Tamar spoke with a certain level of zeal and excitement I hadn't seen in her before. This was the aunt I literally grew up with since both her mother and father, my grandparents, raised me too. I knew Aunty Tamar better than Tiffany and every single one of her friends combined. I knew her from the very first time I opened my eyes to the world, when her parents took me from my biological parents because neither of my parents wanted me then. They thought they were both young to have a child and were in the act of aborting me when my grandmother caught up to my mother and thus saved my life. My grandmother then took me from my mother when I was just a few days old and raised me as her very own child. My aunt and I both grew up under the same roof from that point forward. While her friend Tiffany might be having difficulties believing her, I didn't. I had never before seen Aunt Tamar so alive like when she was sharing what she had referred to as an experiment with Tiffany. One other thing that caught my attention was Aunt Tamar's eyes; they were almost beaming as though they were reflecting burning fire from inside her. That really got my attention, so I closely listened in their conversation.

"What are you talking about, Tamar?"

"You know about my living condition ever since I was having issues with my parents and wanted to move out, right?"

"Right"

"Well, remember that time when I tried to run away from home before I changed my mind?"

"Yes"

"OK, I haven't told anyone about this before. And ... promise you are not going to laugh at me."

"OK, promise! Is everything OK? What really happened?"

"Yes, I am OK. It is just I have thought about it for so long, and every time I found it hard to share my story with anyone, out of fear that I could be laughed at and not believed."

"Trust me; I am not going to laugh at you. I can't promise I would believe you, though, but let's hear you first. OK?" Tiffany said playfully.

"Well, thank you." Then my aunty said something I thought she didn't actually say. "I think God spoke to me."

"Seriously? You mean you actually heard God speak to you?"

"No, it wasn't like that ... And no, I didn't know it was God's voice. I just thought it might have been. Would you stop asking questions and please listen to me?" whispered Aunt Tamar nervously, now speaking in a much softer voice, with her head slightly bent forward in the direction of her friend.

"Ok, I am sorry. Please continue."

"Well, that day when I came to you I was actually crying inconsolably because I had no idea what would happen to me. I was coming to you, but I also knew you couldn't help me since you were still living with your parents as I was. What would become of my future when I had nowhere to go? I was very confused."

"Yes, I remembered, but you came back home that same night, didn't you?"

"Yes, I did. But on my way to your place, when I was venturing in the street crying and trying to locate you for a place to spend the night, I vividly heard someone, a deep voice, talking into my ears and telling me to go back home. I was so afraid, I stopped crying right away. But because I was close to your house anyway, I proceeded forward and found you. That was before I returned home. I just couldn't bring myself to tell you or anyone at the time."

"Wow, really?"

"The scary thing about that incident, I was all alone on the road when it happened. The nearest person was at least half a mile front or back away from me. But that wasn't even what I want to talk to you about."

"Really? What else you want to talk to me about?"

"Ever since that day, after I returned home, I decided on an accidental experiment just because I was confused and in too much pain. I decided to change the way I pray. Well, the first time I did it was sincere, as was every time I got down on my knees to pray, but I didn't intend for it to be an experiment. I want to get that out first, OK?"

"Just get to the point already, what do you mean?"

"Before, in the past, I just prayed however I wanted, once a week, rarely; I even sometime went for months without uttering a single prayer."

"OK."

"On the day of that incident, when I heard a deep voice in my ears, calling me by my name and telling me to return home; it dawned on me that maybe God, if that was his voice, secretly cared for me. As a result, I have decided on a little experiment where I planned on being in a continuous presence with God. Do you see where I am going?"

"Not really."

"Well, you know how some people allocate some time to pray. I wanted to allocate an entire day, or week, or even month just being in a continuous communication before God. You know?"

"Oh girl, seriously? How did that go?"

"For starters, it wasn't that hard. I was just saying short prayers frequently and persistently, regardless of where I was at the time, or even the place. I didn't have any appointed time, and I didn't have any rule. It was as if I was in my father's arms when I was little; you know? I could say anything I wanted, within reason of course. And it felt good. The only thing bad about it was that I couldn't curse or say or do anything bad because he was watching; you know? Just like my father."

"Wow, Tamar, that is very deep. Where did you get that idea from?"

"I told you, it was out of frustration, OK? Anyway, I have discovered something strange. On the days I was in constant communication with God, everything goes well for me. I had peace of mind, no crazy ideas like suicidal thought or even the thought about running from home entered my mind, and I usually got what I wanted. I was actually happy whether I had very little or a lot. That couldn't be a coincidence, right?"

I thought Tiffany noticed it, too; my Aunt Tamar was getting very passionate as she was describing her personal experiment. She was talking with such a conviction, she almost teared up. While Tiffany was still speechlessly staring at her, my Aunt Tamar said something else that not only moved me, but stayed with to me until this day.

"I think God loves me." She said.

She must have seen Tiffany looking in my direction, so she also turned around and saw me. I could tell my aunt was upset at me for snooping on her. Aunt Tamar felt betrayed that I was listening to her private moment with her friend, so she stopped talking and gave me one of those looks, and I left. She might not have intended that information for me, but I took it to heart and have practiced it since, hoping to get the same result. Let me tell you, it works!

That was how I have adopted and practiced the continuous presence before God lifestyle, as compared to a regular or occasional praying lifestyle. It has worked for me, too, in the past. I have used it when I was getting to know the other side of my family, my father and his side of his family. Praying then definitely has helped me, especially with the beating and abuses I have incurred starting just a few short weeks after I met the man who was supposed to be my biological father. My hope was that it would work for me again now as an adult trying to sort out my professional life. A short, one-minute prayer here and there before God the father every little opportunity I got was then my escape; I just couldn't do without. It made me feel connected to God on a more personal level. It was God's vivid presence in my life I felt all the time. It was like my aunt said about 20 years ago, as if God was literally watching me and over me. I felt it.

I didn't tell anyone about Sally and the feeling I had following that phone call she received. Unsure about what to do next, I resumed work and life as usual as if nothing had happened. But when I thought I couldn't discredit my innermost feelings any further, it hit me hard in my stomach and made me feel very uncomfortable. I didn't know what it was, so I did the next best thing and just took a moment to think about it.

As I was thinking, it occurred to me that maybe I was too hard on myself with my daily routine, which was in a small way my disciplinary practice. At that very moment, I had the idea to change something about my routine. But what could it be? I prayed about it and asked God to help me identify areas of my life and daily routine that could benefit from some type of change, any change. As I was thinking and going over the idea in my mind, out of all things, something particularly jumped on me. I tended to park my car, an old Toyota Camry I have been driving for over four years, at the same exact spot every day, and had done for over three years now. It was a nice and shady parking spot under a tree and away from other cars. That was because I liked to sit in it and relax during my lunch hour; plus, I didn't need to worry about anyone scratching my car. I thought that would be easy to change, so I started to park at different and random parking spots every day from that time forward. While I didn't think my other work routine from logging into my computer every morning, checking my work list, checking my emails, getting either coffee or tea in the cafeteria, and actually doing my job needed any change, I tried not to be too predictable. That was how I would come to work sometimes very early, earlier than anyone else, and some other times I would be just on time, while some other times I would run about no more than five or 10 minutes late. I also stopped bringing lunch to work altogether and have never stored food in the work cafeteria's refrigerator. I figured it was fun, and didn't mind a scratched or dented car; so I continued changing up my routine.

Something else changed in the office. My coworker Sally also, on the other hand, seemed to be going through some changes of her own. She seemed to be glowing, and her distinctive walk came back. Sally had the habit of walking on the tip of her toes, or just the balls of her feet, while leaning forward and without letting the entire inside of her feet touch the floor. This gave her the impression of bouncing as though she were about to jump, or fall flat on her face. This was a 50-plus-year-old lady, a mother and a grandmother walking like an insolent high school kid, like a thug. I thought that was odd. Either way, something seemed to have happened to her; whatever it, I could not exactly put my fingers on it.

On about my 12th day of alternating my car parking space and randomly changing up my daily routine, something else happened. I had a strange dream. In my dream, I was transported to my father's house which was in reality, my paternal grandmother's house in the maritime city of Lomé, Togo, somewhere in Africa. That was my birthplace, and where I was conceived, and brought up; my roots. My grandmother's house was a big house built on two adjacent lots, separated by a six-foot-high cement-stone wall. The City of Lomé was a beautiful place with year-round, gorgeous, summer-like weather. It almost was an epiphany of a tropical paradise on Earth with a nice, relaxing and easygoing life. There was always something for everyone to do, tourists and natives alike. A walk on the seashore was one of my favorite things to do. For everyone else, there was the nightlife, the tropical foods, the dance clubs and the clear night sky sprinkled with vibrant and shining stars—so beautiful a thing to look forward to. Together, they offered a much-needed hope to what could be—a tropical city with potential, everyone's favorite destination. As of now, there was practically no worry in the air for everyone; but as for some locals who didn't have any apparent or foreseeable future, the dream of one day leaving their beautiful native land for a better life elsewhere might just have been the only thing keeping them alive. The country's economic situation didn't measure up, and that has opened doors to endless possibilities, and everyone was for himself.

The two-story house painted in light yellow where my grandmother and her children lived was located on the right-hand side of the lot and was commonly referred to as the landlord house. This was because she was the landlord, and that was where she lived. On the other lot were about eight to 10 rental apartments, which served as the main source of income for her. My grandmother was a savvy businesswoman who was very serious about her money. It was her idea to have a reliable source of income, explaining why she built two separate entities of properties on the land she had purchased herself a while back, when the entire place was covered in heavy bushes. The property was one of my grandmother's proudest achievements, she said so herself on more than just a few occasions.

In my dream, I saw Sally nicely dressed in a gray matching silky suit and skirt, walking to my grandmother's house while I was out at the front gate chatting with a couple of my old friends. Sally snubbed me and passed by without greeting or saying a word to me as if she owned the place. I had the urge to stop her because as far I was concerned, Sally has no place there, but I didn't. My eyes slowly followed her as she disappeared behind the red, iron gate. I didn't know what was going on. But because that image disturbed me greatly, I too went through the red, iron gate and into the house after her. I just had to see what brought her there.

The big, iron gate had been purposely painted in red to protect it against corrosion. Red was a popular anti-rust color commonly used for metal doors in that part of the world. On the gate was a painting of a dog in white color; I painted that a long time ago, while I was still living there. It was meant to warn unsuspecting people about a not-so-friendly dog we then had. Sally and I crossed eyes as she was going inside my family house, but she also acted as if she had never seen me before. Once inside the house, Sally directly went into one of my uncle's rooms and sat behind a table that was pre-dressed at the entrance of the door.

That was Uncle Tito's room. Uncle Tito was my father's older biological brother who, unlike the rest of my uncles, wasn't a nice man. While him and my father both shared the same parents, mother and father; that was where their similarity ended. My grandmother was a bit promiscuous during her younger years; she had children with two different lovers. She had four children with my grandfather before moving on, and had three other children with another man. That was all I knew. If she was in some kind of relationship with anyone else, I was not made aware of it. Either way, Uncle Tito was the firstborn of her marriage with my grandfather; Aunt Sylvania was the second; Christopher, my father, was the third; and Aunt Adele the last. After my grandfather, my grandmother got married to another man by whom she had three additional children. Uncle Richard was the first born of that union, fifth overall; Uncle Tom was the second and sixth overall; and Aunt Samantha third and seventh overall. My grandfather wasn't exactly a saint, either; in fact, he had done the worst. As an aspiring medical doctor traveling around the country wherever he was needed, my grandfather, I was told, had fathered many children with many different women. His profession brought him both fame and fortune, and of course as many as 20-plus children, thanks to other marriages. Polygamy, though not preferred, was then acceptable in that part of the world. While the family was never able to locate all of my grandfather's children or ex-wives after his passing, everyone has tried to accept things for what they were and lived together in complete harmony.

Sally going into Uncle Tito's room with a table dressed before her right across the entrance door was a very bad sign, even in a dream. That was because Tito was not a very nice man; he was into witchcraft, voodoo, black magic and sorcery. It was a well-known fact around the house that Tito did some questionable things in his past. It was also a known story that Tito might have stolen his younger brother Christopher's good fortune (that would be my father) through black magic or witchcraft. While no one actually knew what he did exactly, what everyone knew was what they actually saw him do. Tito factually forced his younger brother to eat an entire pigeon whole, all while being locked in a room for an entire day. The drenching thing about that whole story was that the pigeon might have been used in voodoo sacrifice of some sort. Tito had also slapped his own mother, and this, in front of everybody when she tried to intervene on his younger brother Christopher's behalf. This was an utter disgrace; it was an abomination to say the least, yet no one dared do anything about it.

They were all afraid of Tito. My mother, while recounting the story, added that I was less than a year old when it all happened. Timing was very important, thanks to my unannounced arrival and the anxiety that I brought forth with me into this world. What should have been a celebration turned out to be a troubling time for my father and his family, who would have preferred me dead than alive. And even my own mother, who was not so innocent for almost not having me, couldn't fully comprehend the magnitude of what was going on at the time. Decisions were consciously made, and it came to pass.

While I did not see Tito in my dream, I was certain there were some sort of relationship between him and Sally. What would she be doing in his room if they weren't somehow connected? I neither understood nor liked that combination. Plus, I knew that room. It had been vacant since I met my father for the first time at the tender age of 9, a few months shy of my 10th birthday. During that time, Tito was on a long business trip abroad, working in another country. He only came home every two or three years, sometimes longer.

Uncle Tito's room was right behind that of my father on the first floor of the two-story house. My grandmother had rented out the upper level for top dollar to some Nigerian businesspeople who were rarely home. They did remember to pay their rent ahead of time, or my grandmother would have kicked them out a long time ago. Anyway, my grandmother and family lived on the first floor. My father occupied the smaller room: a studio room in the right corner of the building directly facing the red, iron gate door, and Tito the second angle room right behind my father's room. Tito's room was directly facing the bathroom outside, separated by a passageway that led to the iron-gate door.

Tito, who was a self-proclaimed Christian convert, exhibited no shyness or hesitation when talking about his past, especially his involvement and knowledge in the area of black magic. Before that, Tito was everything he claimed to be. Just by listening to him talk, it was easy to see that Tito was not only arrogant, he had also sought riches, power and many other things though dark magic in his younger days. One time, while Tito was away in a different country for work, my cousin Peter, who was Aunt Adele's son, and I ventured into Tito's room by accident, before curiosity got the best of us. What we saw scared us for a very long time. It was scary, repulsive and repugnant. We saw, in between thick spider webs, small idols and animal skulls in the open. Those were black magic stuff. There were also mammal skulls on tables, under the tables, along the wall. We also saw small clay idols adorned with birth feathers, gooey dripping red substance and white powdery substances. This is the room of someone who went around telling people, he converted to Christianity. We immediately ran out and closed the door behind us as quickly as we were able. The room was smelly and repulsive, and left us with an unpleasant memory which we desperately tried to forever erase from our mind. This happened when I was a child, and I have not forgotten.

Seeing Sally in that very room was very alarming to me. What could she be doing there? I didn't need to look much further to see a line of people started to form from outside the iron gate, now wide open all the way to Uncle Tito's door. Sally was selling flowers. The very beautiful flowers I had seen exposed near the gate on the floor stacked up against and atop the dividing wall were what she planned on selling. Those flowers were gorgeous, nice, lively and beautiful in a variety of colors. Some of the flowers were in plastic vases, some in cement vases, while others were in clay vases. They were all flamboyant and wonderfully dressed. I was able to recognize flowers such as mums, or chrysanthemums in various colors, but predominantly in yellow and bright orange colors blossoming from the ground all the way to the top of the six-foot wall separating my family's property from the neighbor's.

There were also roses of a variety of colors: red, rose, yellow and white, and other beautiful flowers I didn't know existed and couldn't possibly recognize by name. The entire set was magnificently amazing. I was more than stunned; I was shocked, dumbfounded and confused at the same time. Sally's customers were some local people who seemed eager for their turn, or a signal of some sort to pay for the flower arrangements they so desired to take them home with them. While none of the locals actually bought any of the flowers and walked away with them, they were there and ready to start the transaction. I knew deep inside my heart Sally didn't belong there; and those flowers were not hers to sell. Uncle Tito couldn't possibly have known Sally; he never traveled to the United States and didn't work for the same company for which Sally and I were working. How they knew each other was a complete mystery. Either way, she had to go.

Confused and furious about what was actually taking place before my very eyes, I felt the urge to vent my anger somewhere else, somewhere where I always felt free. So I got into my father's room and changed into my soccer gear, my black shorts with white stripes on each side, a white T-shirt and short socks with a pair of running shoes. I was ready to go to the park, where I was certain to find people playing the sport we all loved. Many things were going through my mind. While I was getting ready to head out to process that information and weight my options, something suddenly caught my attention. The sand was slowly shifting before my eyes, giving way to something. I didn't know what it was, but I also knew it couldn't be good. Awakening from the dirt sand right before my eyes while I was still standing on my father's porch was a dark green, lean and long snake—longer than the one I had seen in my previous dream which had Sally's face. The snake was mysteriously rising up above the ground as in a science fiction movie, as would a helicopter, except it was still dormant and wasn't moving at all. Its eyes were still shut.

When it reached knee level, it started to shock itself, which caused the sands and dirt to fall off its body. It then started to stretch as if awakened from a long sleep. My good sense told me to run; the snake was getting ready to fly and bite someone. Snakes were not supposed to be doing that! And if my intuition were right, I knew something bad was about to happen. All of a sudden, the Sally presence in the house and inside Uncle Tito's room started to make sense. I was able to connect the dots. But before the snake could open its eyes, I took off like a rocket at full speed, as I have done numerous times on the soccer pitch as a forward. I was the striker and would not be slow. Moreover, I would not stay around and let any snake, or that one, strike me. I thanked God for my active wear. The snake flew after me, as expected.

The chase was on. I zipped through the crowd of Sally's potential customers, and none of them seemed even remotely bothered by what was going on. They were as baffled about me running in and around them as I was of them not knowing what was going on. It was as if I were the only one who could see the flying snake; it was probably too fast for their eyes. I turned around, and the snake was still at my tail and didn't even bother to bite any of them. Wow! The snake must have been awakened just for me; it has locked in on me. Was I that special for someone to have gone through all that trouble to harm me? I couldn't run a straight line; it was going to gain ground on me. So I quickly zig zagged through the line of people a few different times til I lost sight of it. I must have lost the flying snake, for it was nowhere to be found. So the idea then came to me to run into my father's room, which I did.

I then closed the door behind me and quickly looked around for a weapon. I was lucky to find a big, sizeable wooden stick. I picked it up and held it up high with both hands, knowing that the flying snake would eventually find me; only this time I had something with which to work. I quickly and quietly waited out the snake for about a long five minutes, and when I thought it wouldn't come, there it was slowly slipping its slender body through the gap under the door and into my father's room. And so I rained down on it—the most vicious and savage beating my body was capable of delivering on that snake. I beat it flat to the cemented floor. I swung the bat so violently, so repeatedly and so fast, my body began to drench in its own sweat. I continued to rain the beating down on it until my white T-shirt became completely soaked wet in my own sweat. I beat it, beat it and beat it some more, but the snake wouldn't die. Flattened on the floor, it started to do something normal snakes are accustomed to doing.

Instead of flying, it started to slowly crawl forward, but at a snail pace on its abdomen. Now the entire house could hear me and came into the door, and watched and saw the snake they weren't able to see just a moment earlier. I had revealed it with my utmost severe beatings. Some people, the women, started to shout, but I did not relent; I kept the beatings going. The snake couldn't die, but it sure felt the pain. I was right on top of it with every inch it gained forward with my repeated blows. A single one of my blows would have been enough to kill and immobilize a small mammal like a rabbit or a raccoon, but not that snake. Between the noises of the spectators and every single one of my blows, the resilient and seemingly immortal snake slowly advanced til it reached a small hole in the corner of my father's room. Unbeknownst to me, there was a hole connecting both my father's room and that of Tito. Everyone saw the snake as it slowly crawled on its way and disappeared in it.

It was gone; the flying snake has vanished into the small black hole and would have certainly gone to Tito's room. Then I heard my Aunt Samantha, who happened to be among the spectators, say to me.

"Acid, pour liquid acid into the hole; it would kill the snake." But I had no liquid acid.

"Where do find liquid acid?" I asked in an urgent voice.

"Uncle Tito's room; he has some." She responded.

So I quickly got outside at full speed and ran toward Uncle Tito's room, only to be stopped at the entrance door by a road block. Sally was the only one who didn't budge. In fact, she didn't even try to come and see for herself why everyone was yelling in the room next door, or what the noises were about. She didn't bother to want to know why I was in a sweat, or why I still had the big wooden stick in my hand. But she successfully stopped me from getting in Uncle Tito's room. I raised my head to see if Uncle Tito was inside, but it was dark in there and I wasn't able to see him or anything for that matter. Deeply disappointed and madly frustrated, I returned to my father's room with a plan to seal that hole with cement. That also marked the end of the show, and the locals, who just a few minutes earlier lined up to buy flowers from

Sally, were no longer interested. They slowly started to leave the house, while I stood on the porch of my father's room with the wooden rod still in my right hand, until the last one of them closed the red, iron gate behind him.

That was when I woke up. It was around two in the morning. I went to use the bathroom and brushed my teeth before getting down my knees for a few minutes. In my prayer, I thanked God for everything he was doing in my life like I always did. I also thanked him for protecting me and winning the battle for me.

I went to work the next day as though nothing happened. That was when I noticed something else; something had knocked the wind out of Sally's walk. She didn't walk on her toes; she walked like a regular person. It took me til the end of the day to notice. That was when I started to really connect what I thought were some noteworthy dots. Who or what Sally exactly was, I would probably never know; I didn't plan on it. But twice I have seen her in my dream, and both times she was associated with a snake that tried to bite me. The first time, she was the big fat snake that tried to ambush me; I barely escaped her when she launched at me. The second time, she found a way to my root; I was sure to find out about my origin—who I was, and how she could take me out. Uncle Tito might have offered to help her, or she would not be having a table set at the entrance door to his room.

Uncle Tito was not a nice man. He was, in fact, an evil man who once slapped his own mother, and if what the locals were secretly murmuring was true, he stole my father's good fortune through black magic. If my analogy was thorough, then those beautiful flowers I had seen in my dream must belong to me. For all I know, they could symbolize something positive in my life, or even my future. If the flowers are a symbolic representation of my future and were indeed mine, then I can see why someone like Sally would want to sabotage them; they are beautiful and she is an evil person who hates me. Unfortunately, I cannot afford to let her or anyone else for that matter, take them from me, not even in a dream. I am a blessed child of God. Last time I checked, what God blesses no one can ever curse. I am equally sure he won't let anybody rob me of his blessings in my life.

After that incident, I have become so much more thoughtful and conscientious about my prayer life. It was no surprise that I doubled down on it. I have prayed so much and so constantly I can't remember a moment gone by without me uttering thanksgiving praise to the Lord. That was how I literally and rightfully committed everything to God, for I sincerely believe he has saved me. I also believed whatever happened to me, only served to strengthen my faith and make me a much better person. I felt humbled and much more appreciative for everything I have gone through, and the new perspective it has given me on pretty much everything. I might not have been happy about both Sally and Tito, but I didn't hold any grudge against them. I have forgiven them; that was what the Bible taught us. I have also prayed for them, hoping that God would turn their heart around and save them too. If God first loved us regardless of our sins, and gave us a roadmap to eternal life through the grace of Jesus Christ, I was sure they too could be saved so long as they are willing to turn to him.

CHAPTER 11

The Three Handicaps That Almost Stalled the Plane

The Enemy's Final Attempt to Terrify and to Destroy

W hile I was fast asleep, I had yet another vision. This time, I had become a vibrant young entrepreneur traveling through the city of Chicago for a very important business meeting. This meeting represented a once-in-a-lifetime opportunity for me to pitch my ideas for a major business venture. In the dream it felt like a very exciting moment in my life, which it seemed I had been looking forward to for a very long time. I had worked very hard to get the opportunity and elements in the right place that led me to that meeting. I was ready, and every fiber in my athletic and fit body told me this was my time. If successful, the venture would revive and rejuvenate my career and give me a complete new direction and outlook on life. It wasn't like any other meeting I had ever had. This was a crossroads in the journey of my life …

I lost the software development role at the young technology firm close to where I was living at the time in New York. I loved that job because of its convenience, and also because it offered a decent enough pay to support my small family. More than anything, it paid the bills. I won't lie to you: I took that loss very hard. Sometime even the most resilient of people find it difficult to bounce back from some of the harsh disappointments of life. But I tried not to let it define me. So I quickly but painfully swallowed my pride and decided to see the good in it.

What could have possibly been the bright side of losing my job? Well, now I had more time to myself, which was good. I could now catch up with my family and spend some time with my son, whom I barely had any time to play with before when I had a job. It was a position I held for nearly a year, and I had grown attached to friends I made while I was there. And whereas I sincerely loved the company and the people I had the honor and privilege to meet and work alongside, things just did not work out between the company and me.

Some things, I guessed, were not meant to be. So I had to move on. The lack of family time or work-life balance, and the tremendous amount of stress that came with that territory, had everything to do with it. Nevertheless, it still was a tough decision to make. For once, it meant no more reliable source of income at least until I found another job. In the face of it all, I had to stay strong, remain positive and make all the right decisions for what could also be a once-in-a-lifetime's opportunity to take a long and hard look at myself and my career, and take corrective actions. I was determined now, more so than ever, to make the best out of this situation, my situation. For once, I was going to get a much-needed rest. I was also going to take my time and reposition myself for the current job market's demands. Everything was just going to be great.

I knew there were a lot of demands for my type of profession, so I was not concerned about whether or not I was going to find something reasonable that was going to allow me some time with my family. It was just a matter of time. As an application developer with a broad technical background with many years of experience, and having worked as an Application Developer, a Technical Support Specialist, an Application Support Analyst, a Software Developer specializing in Microsoft Dot Net Technologies and a Systems Analyst specializing in reporting and all things databases, I felt very good about my odds at getting back to work rather quickly. But on the other hand, I also didn't want to get back in the saddle too quickly. I needed this time off, which I considered a blessing in disguise, almost like an unexpected vacation, to help me catch my breath and refresh myself. That was my long-term career future, and most importantly my overall well-being and peace of mind. As for now, the moment was for me to take, to soak myself in and to not have any regret. I would try my very best to make the best of it, arguably the best pre-retirement vacation I would probably get in my entire life. What was not to like about that?

I was not concerned about my career path, for while I knew I was not in any way perfect and had made a few mistakes here and there, who hadn't? No one ever said the road to success was without obstacles or detours. They happen to everyone, and they have happened to me. What they didn't do was stop me from pursuing my goals and aspirations. And I am thankful; in fact, I consider myself very fortunate. This is because not everyone was as lucky as I was: having to work my way up from nothing, from a very humble upbringing. No matter how difficult things were and no matter the number of times life knocked me down, I somehow, someway come back stronger, hungrier, and more determined. If that wasn't a blessing, I have no idea what a blessing is. That much I know with an absolute certainty. While I might not have been lucky at some junctions of life, I knew my worth, and I also knew my materials, what I had to bring to the table.

But since I could soon be getting back on my feet to go out to work, I just wanted to enjoy this moment, for it might not come back again. In between, I also planned on reeducating myself, to get better, smarter, more informed and sharper so I would be returning to the workforce better than when I had exited it. Surprisingly enough, many things had changed in the job market in a small space of time. For instance, interviews and application processing were no longer conducted the way they once were nearly a decade ago. The age of technology was definitely upon us by then, and it successfully affected many lives and landscapes alike, with the job market being one of them. I was just blessed to be living right in the eye of that good storm. For my part, it was perfect timing.

In the past, I learned things the old-fashioned way, by trial and error. Not anymore. Unfortunately for me, that approach no longer worked. Many companies nowadays didn't have patience, and it also seemed they were only looking for candidates who could instantly identify and solve their problems. As a result, I figured a complete revamp of my overall technical skillset was in order. If I was to become a better software developer, or anything else in that line of work, if I were to succeed, I had to be ready for everything and anything. Besides, all I needed to succeed was a good supportive environment and a good home where I could be allowed to put my technicality to practice. Although a shoot-first, ask-questions-later approach of resolving technical problems might have resolved the immediate problem in the past with some of my previous employers, that clearly was not the right way to do things now. Still, that was what many technology firms wanted out of their employees. They seemed only concerned about solving the immediate problems right there and now, and fast, without much thought into the future. It went without saying that was not the most realistic or time-effective way to address modern-day technology and related issues. Either way, because that was what most companies wanted, that was what I too must prepare myself to deliver. I might not have been a magician, but a genius; that was easy. In fact, a genius was exactly what I was, am, and had to become; there was no middle ground, as I could not afford to be anything else.

Meanwhile, still in my dream, there was a huge delay with my connecting flight at O'Hare International Airport, forcing a multitude of travelers, myself included, to wait indefinitely. Frustrated, I decided to momentarily leave the airport perimeter for fresh air, in my attempt to get away from the maddening chaos; and I did. While I was still outside of the airport vicinity, walking, I saw an old friend of mine, Stephane, with his girlfriend walking their small dog. They stopped at the sight of me.

"Hi Stephane, how are you?"

"I am good Dee; what are you doing all the way here?"

"I am traveling through your city, and thanks for asking. Please allow me to return the same question; you don't live here now, do you?"

"Yes, I do, with my girlfriend Hillary." With that, Stephane turned around and introduced us. "Dee, meet Hillary; Hillary, meet Dee, an old friend of mine."

"Nice to meet you, Dee," said Hillary with a smile.

"Nice to meet you as well, Hillary, and thank you for taking such great care of my good friend Stephane," I said with smile. To this, Hillary flashed a wider smile and continued:

"I think Stephane is doing a good job taking care of himself, but you are welcome anyway." At this we all casually laughed. We went on to engage in small talk for a few minutes until we each seemed to be running out of things to talk about.

"Oh wow, Dee, time has flown, you know?" added Stephane, now checking his wrist. I could tell he needed to leave.

"Yes, it has, it certainly has," I said. At this, Hillary leaned over and whispered something into Stephane's ears.

"Dee, I really wish we could hang out more some other time in a café, my place or some other more convenient place. When are you leaving the city?"

"I don't know, in a few hours maybe, as soon as the airlines decide to let us board the plane, I guess." Then I looked at Hillary and Stephane, because it was obvious they had someplace to be and did not want to be late. "You guys must be busy; and I am very sorry for holding you up."

"As a matter of fact, we need to meet up with a friend in exactly half an hour."

"It is great bumping into to you, and Hillary, it is a pleasure to meet you." At this, Stephan turned around and shook my hand.

"Bye Dee, and have a nice flight. I do hope they get you to your destination safe and hopefully on time," said Stephane before turning to his girlfriend. They both continued walking their dog in the opposite direction.

"Thank you," I replied.

While I was more than happy to share with Stephane and Hillary my agony, having to wait on my connecting flight that just would not take off for a very long time, I was nevertheless glad to see them. And that would not have happened if my flight weren't delayed. About 20 minutes later, I found my way back to the airport terminal and realized that I did not have my passport with me. I didn't need it while I was boarding my flight back in New York; my driver's license was enough. All of the sudden they were asking me for a passport I didn't have with me in the first place. It was a complete shock to me. *I should have taken that stinking passport and avoided having to answer the same question over and over again,* I thought to myself. Good thing they didn't make a big deal out of it, either, as I was not traveling outside of the country. My driver's license was again enough for the flight attendant to authenticate me and communicate my seat number on the flight that just would not take off.

The airplane had long arrived and was parked at the edge of the tarmac. Everyone could see it. What we did not understand was what was wrong with it, and why wouldn't anyone communicate that information to us. Maybe the plane had some mechanical problem, or maybe there were other problems the airline company couldn't afford to share with the passengers, out of fear it could hurt their image and reputation. We had been waiting for hours; fatigue and frustration were slowly beginning to get to everyone.

Just when we thought things could not get any worse, out of nowhere came three disabled individuals dragging themselves on the floor. Slowly but steadily, they made their way through the security checkpoint, and no one, not even the security guards or the two police officers standing nearby, even attempted to stop them or ask them a question. The disabled individuals did not show any proof of identification and were not even searched like everyone else. What was even more bizarre was the simple fact that security guards did not even look at them. Must they not have seen the three dirty and physically handicapped individuals; I later learned were not people at all, but rather spirits, dragging themselves on the surface of the floor right in front of them? Could they not smell the foul smell emanating from the three handicaps, so strong and so repulsive enough to cause anyone close enough to vomit?

On second thought, a few other people, and not just I, were paying attention to them. I knew this because some passengers were beginning to get up from their seats and looking at each other and in the direction of the slowly moving, repulsive individuals. By the look of everyone's faces, it seemed only a handful of people could actually see them. Why was it that only some people could see them, while others could not? I sincerely had no idea. The three disabled men were confident and did not seem bothered by anyone at all. While the odor coming from them seemed loaded with irritating particles—it was already making it hard for some people to breathe—that did not slow them down; they kept moving forward, and no one actually attempted to stop them. A lot of passengers covered their nose and mouth with whatever was closest to them; some used the blanket they were covering themselves with, others used their shirts while others used the palm of their hands. The smell was that strong in the air, now polluted.

Everyone was literally in a state of disarray as the three disabled white men in their mid-40s to early 50s slowly and grotesquely, made their way uninterrupted through the terminal gate, as if they were about to board the plane outside—a plane no one was able to board for the past six plus hours. No one dared say a word to them; no one was even sure whether they were all seeing things, or if whatever they were seeing was actually happening. And, unlike the passengers waiting, none of the three disabled men were carrying any luggage or anything with them, which made it hardly believable that they would, in fact, board a plane that would not fly. Curious, I, and as many as a third of all waiting passengers, got on our feet and stared at them painfully crawling their way through the glass door separating the terminal from the tarmac outside, one by one. Then something completely unexpected happened! As soon as the disabled men made it outside, they literary transfigured themselves into some sort of unknown, four-legged beasts with a giant head, strong muscular body and a short tail.

The three disabled, who could barely move across the floor just a moment ago, were literally and suddenly transformed into some fast, sprinting and almost flying beasts that could scale and climb any building faster than anything I had ever seen in my entire life up until that day. They were literally flying up the building. Their faces morphed into that of a male baboon with a massive head, about two or three times that of normal baboons. Their mouths were equipped with four long, dagger-like and very intimidating fangs. Their body was that of a very muscular hyena with four very muscular legs. At the extremities of each of their four paws were some of the longest and strongest claws I have ever seen before on any living creature. Their claws were so strong; they literally left their imprints, which were puncture marks and open gashes, behind them. The beasts were enormous, ferocious, intimidating and were nothing like anything I had ever seen before in my entire life.

At the sight of this, everyone ran for cover. Those who could fit under desks squeezed themselves under; those who were fortunate enough to find an open office or small hidden places were far too happy to quickly hide themselves. The transfigured beasts immediately devised a tactic and spread out as soon as they gained some altitude. One beast went on top of the plane outside, jumping up and down on top of it as if to claim it, and thus making it nearly impossible for anyone to go near the plane, let alone board it. The second beast went on top of the airport building, as if to hold the entire airport hostage, and I was running back and forth. Its job was to survey the place, and it was getting very aggressive at anything—cars and people alike—moving or getting even remotely close to the building. The third and final beast was in charge of the inside job. It actually found its way back into the terminal through an opening in the ceiling. Once inside, it did not get down; it stayed up in the vaulted ceiling. It was aggressively jumping up and down between the building's supporting beams in the ceiling, scaring everyone—passengers and airport employees—on sight.

The three beasts were no clueless disabled men after all; they could have been some disguised evil spirit for all I knew. They were very coordinated and seemed to know exactly what they each needed to do. They were on a mission. But what mission? It seemed they were coordinating efforts to ground and stop the planes from flying. But why? There were thousands of planes at many different airports throughout the entire nation, but why only this one? Maybe it was someone they were trying to prevent from boarding this particular plane. Obviously! They were also trying to prevent anyone from the outside from helping the helpless hostages inside. Definitely! As if that weren't enough, they were similarly trying to control the helpless hostages already inside. The three beasts did something else together; they were all making some horrendous noises while jumping up and down and showing their dagger-like fangs. It was a terrifying sight, and no one dared look at the beast in the ceiling—no one but me.

I knew there was much more to the scene than met the eyes, so I cautiously docked by the ticket station where I checked myself in a little while ago. My mind was racing a million miles an hour. I had already looked up and located the beast when it momentarily dropped down mid-height to terrify someone who had just moved. I didn't lie down flat on my belly like most people were, while covering their eyes in complete submission to the beasts. It seemed those were the only people the beasts were not bothering; they were safe as long as they did not move or look upward.

I knew the three beasts could be defeated. If only I could put my hands on some sort of weapon, and a way to carry that out. The only visible weapons in sight were the guns the two visible police officers long passed out had on them. Although they were face-up on the ground, as though dead, there was no possible way for me to get to them without being spotted by the beast in the ceiling. *How could I get the guns without being seen by the beast?* Suppose the beast in the ceiling sees me in my attempt to get to the guns. *Were they powerful enough to kill or at least injure it?* There was only one way to find that out. If I were going to make any type of move, I definitely needed some sort of distraction; and those guns had better fire on the first squeeze of the trigger. *What were my other options?* As my mind was working really fast to figure a way to quickly kill these beasts before they caused injury, or worse, killed anyone, I tried to carefully locate the beast in the ceiling. It should be in about my nine o'clock, right above my right shoulder, in the midsession of the ceiling. It had just come down not too long ago to ferociously scare a woman whose baby began to cry. She had quickly succeeded at quieting the baby by cuddling the crying baby while covering his mouth the entire time.

Just as I was thinking we might be in a no-win battle, something else happened, when I discreetly tried to check for the beast's exact location in the ceiling before deciding whether or not I should run for the guns. The beast and I accidentally crossed eyes, and it abruptly made some squeamish noise. But that was not all; unlike for everyone else, it also did not drop down from the ceiling to scare me. I knew something happened when the beast temporarily looked me in the eyes. It saw something that frightened it. *Did some kind of mysterious power just come out of my eyes and scare this ferocious-looking beast? It saw something in my eyes; but what did it see?* I had no fear in my eyes; maybe that was what it saw. Either way, I did not budge. *What could the beast possibly have seen in my eyes?* I did not know, but it added to my confidence level, emboldening me and making me believe now more than ever that I could take it on and win. And the beast knew it.

That was all I needed. So I raised my head and looked up, but the beast was too afraid to now look me in the eyes. That was when I got up tall on my feet to face it, counting on nothing and none but God, my deliverer. Right at that very moment, I too could feel my body going through some type of transformation on its own, from my inside out. There was an actual ball of fire slowly growing inside of me. I could vividly see it in my mind and feel it in my gut getting bigger and bigger, with every breath I took. Even though I could not see the fire, heat and smoke were literally coming out of the openings of my nose, mouth and ears. I was literally fuming from my inside out and could have set anything on fire by just touching it. I was generating enough energy to consume the entire place, yet I was not burning.

All of a sudden it occurred to me: maybe that was what the beast in the ceiling saw when it looked into my eyes, a ball of fire. At that point, I had no need for any gun. I did not even need any weapon to stop those beasts. I mysteriously became the ultimate weapon none of the beasts could put out. They would spontaneously combust if they dared get anywhere near me. This also explains why the beast in the ceiling retreated to the furthest corner of the ceiling and didn't dare getting near me.

The once ferocious beast was now shivering uncomfortably and uncontrollably in the ceiling—too scared to even find an escape route … That was when I woke up from my sleep. I quickly got up from the bed and went to the bathroom, where I cleaned my face and brushed my teeth. I came back and knelt by the same bed and said a brief thanksgiving prayer for a few long minutes. I then returned to bed and almost forgot I ever had that dream in the first place.

I woke up the next day; and I kept remembering specifics about that strange dream I had. It felt as if it were an incident I lived, and that there were some beasts after me. So I meditated on it, hoping to find some connection. While I did not know what the three beasts were or who sent them, if anybody sent them, and if their real mission was to prevent me from boarding the plane. I knew there had to be some sort of meaning to the dream. Every dream has a meaning. My first thought was, wow, someone hated me so much and decided to persecute me. If I were right, someone had been working extra hours and hard just to see me fail and keep me in a constant state of fear. But I was not afraid, for I knew I had the spirit of the living God in me, protecting me and helping me overcome things I normally should not overcome. With him in my corner, no enemy of mine has a chance. I felt as though the power of God working in me was all they could see; maybe that was why I was able to defeat the beast in my dream without ever lifting a finger. Whoever was behind the beasts might have been lurking behind me for an opportune time to strike. But who could that possibly be? I could not think about anyone who hated me that much. In fact, I did not have any enemy I could name. Just that moment, I remembered something strange that happened to me a couple of weeks prior to me having that vision.

While I was still unemployed and trying to enjoy my unexpected non-vacation vacation time, I received a text message from someone who claimed to be a representative of a specific company who wanted to hire me for a software development job opening. It was around nine o'clock in the morning, and I'd just gotten out of bed. Whereas it was very odd for any company to text anyone they have not met before for an employment opportunity, I decided to take the chance and replied anyway. After all, this is the 21st century. Tech companies should probably be trying to utilize technology to recruit their candidates the best way they know how; maybe texting was becoming the new norm. Most companies preferred sending email or directly calling their prospective candidates. The text message simply stated:

"Good morning, Mr. DeeRoy." I noticed the person spelled my name correctly. He must have known me or had my résumé in front of them.

"Good morning, may I know who this is?" I replied awhile later. The person at the other end provided me with a hyperlink and recommended I apply to a job for which they thought I was an ideal candidate. Only when I clicked on the hyperlink, it redirected me to another page with the message "it works" on it. I was being mocked!

I quickly looked up the company the pretend recruiter said he or she was representing. I then located the company's career site, copied that link and sent it to him in a reply text message with the following message with a smiley face: "The correct URL (web address) would have been the URL I sent." I then concluded by saying, "If this is a known wicked person who is rejoicing over my downfall, here is a riddle for you: 'The Lord Almighty did not forget or forsake him [his creation, meaning me] during his moment of distress. In due time, he who made both the heaven and Earth would raise him up high well above any planet known to mankind, and shine his glory upon him for all to see. ☺'" I then copied the telephone number that was being used and looked it up online. It was a fake Internet number that could not be traced. So I was validated, and the person did not respond back to me. Someone was indeed rejoicing over my shortcoming, and that really disturbed me. Because random people did not just text people they did not know ahead of time to prank, this person definitely knew me from somewhere. The prankster also knew that I did not have any job at the time. But who, and from where?

The only names that came to mind were Sally Voursheer, and Katrina Jones. I could not believe it. I could not remember having any disagreement with anyone else, nor had I offended anyone in recent memory. It had been nearly a year since I left that company, the last known place where I actually had a disagreement with someone. Sally and Katrina, my ex-colleague and manager who wanted me dead because I dared speak my mind on some particular projects we worked on together in the past. They were still after me and definitely had their hands in that prank. They had a motive; they knew my phone number and an inside connection to my next company after I left them.

While I did not know that information while I was exchanging text messages with them, something did come over me. I did not even know what I was texting, or what it even meant. I only recalled goose bumps all over my body, as a chilly sensation traversed my entire body from head to toes. I was visibly upset; that I knew. What I did not know was why I responded the way I did. I did not recall when I clicked the send button, but I regretted sending that last message as soon as I came back to my senses. Either way, that person did not respond back, which confirmed my suspicion. I could have looked up the web address the person sent me to find out what server it came from, but I did not think it was worth my time. So I let it go and completely forgot about it.

Things started to click soon after. My strange dream and that prank were most definitely related; I could tell. I could not bring myself to accept they were completely unrelated coincidences. If someone actually went through that trouble just to see me fail, and turn around and rub it in my face. That was low and evil. And only a handful of people are capable of things of that nature. It seemed my enemies desperately wanted me to miss my connecting flight; my life must then have a tremendous significance. I must be so important that they felt the need to deploy not one, not two, but three ferocious beasts just to ground me, make me miss my meeting, sabotage my life and rejoice over my downfall? That is just outrageous and plain evil.

Sure, I regretted replying to that text message. Informing a wicked person who was literally rejoicing over my shortcomings that my better days are ahead of me was not the smartest thing to do. He or she might try to prevent those better days from happening, provided they had the means to do it and they were motivated enough to bring that about. I realized this. At the same time, the spirit within me did not think it was a good idea to let whomever that prankster was rejoice over my misfortune. So I let that person know that my slip-up was not the end of me.

I implied that I was going to rise again, higher, bigger and brighter than I ever was. While I believed this with all my heart, that was a piece of information I would rather keep to myself. Oh, how I wished I had better control over my instinct and the spirit that moved within me. No good usually came from telling something like that to a complete stranger. In fact, in the book of Genesis, one particular biblical character by the name of Joseph had a dream about his future and told the very people he loved and trusted the most, his own family; and it didn't work out so well for him.

> "And Joseph dreamed a dream, and he told it his brothers: and they hated him yet the more."
> —Genesis 37:5 (King James Version)

That was when I realized what a drastic mistake I had made, even though I didn't even have any dreams about my future, like Joseph did. I simply had an intuition, and already I went about telling a total and complete stranger at the other end who was actually mocking my shortcoming. It was no wonder they sent the three beasts at me.

My unexpected blessing in disguise turned out to be a three-month long restful and productive vacation I wasn't expecting, and I wouldn't have gotten otherwise. It was by far the longest vacation of my life. During that time, I caught up with my family, whom I rarely spent any time with beforehand. I also did a total and complete revamp of myself and my career objectives. I took some much-needed technical online courses in my effort to update my skillsets. I again felt ready for the job market. I applied to a few hundred jobs in that timeframe, and went to a few unsuccessful interviews. As if by design, I received not one, but two good offers, with a pending third offer only after my wife and I welcomed our baby daughter into the world. God is simply great! I have since started a new phase of my life working as a System Analyst at a great, local company where I felt right at home on day one. I know with an absolute certainty, everything that has happened to me thus far in life has prepared me for this very moment.

I am eternally grateful, for the Lord has protected and blessed me through it all. As a result, I didn't miss any of my flights, or my connecting flights.

CHAPTER 12

Overcoming From Within

How to Win the Right Way – From the Inside Out

We might have been created in the perfect image of God, but that is not how we see ourselves most of the time. Our very lives, thoughts and deeds can testify to that. This explains why we constantly strive to better ourselves. We do this to try and become a better version of ourselves today than we were yesterday. In that light, we are continuously trying to refine ourselves in any and every way.

We are, in fact, a perpetually refining breed of creature, and not just any creature: we are human beings, the finest ever created. We have an innate desire to keep improving who we are, what we do and how we do it by continuously learning and applying lessons learned in areas we deem fit and convenient to us, because we can. This is because we have the liberty, the freedom, the control within our grasp and the privilege to do so.

So we learn from our own mistakes and the mistakes of others and try to use that information to our advantage and toward the never-ending redefining jobs of improvements. As humans, we also don't cease to come up with new and improved ways and methodologies to better just about everything we do. Everything that comes in contact with us, and everything we touch, we have an effect on. We are, to say the least, a resilient bunch that feels the need to reach higher and higher, even though the ultimate highest point has not yet been defined. And that is what sets us apart from the other creatures. We all have the need to face and do the impossible within us, in our heart; and all we sometimes need is a spark.

All we sometimes need is a chance, an encounter, a dream, a revelation or a struggle that serves as the catalyst that can launch us into a different realm that may change our lives for the better. We were born to be challenged, to be motivated, to seek. We can afford to take the chance to try just a little harder or differently than before. And we are okay with that. In fact, we will often regret not taking certain chances even if we knew the probability of a failure has been predicted. In that case, we might realize all we needed was the experience. So the truth is that we find joy and fulfillment in the process of doing something, and not necessarily in the aftermath.

The stimulus that may be needed for someone to change the world can come in many forms. It might be something as little as just having the right tools or being in the right place and at the right time, and also being faced with a sufficient enough challenge forcing us to try just a little bit harder. Who would have thought that telling someone he or she can't do something would end up being the catalyst that changed that person's life? It has always struck me as funny the expressions "you can't," "you can't do this," "you can't do that," "you can't reach this," "you can't reach that." All of which basically are ways of saying "you're not good enough," and are often the best single motivational spark with which one can be induced. The words can set in motion the actions of an individual to achieve an eventual greatness, or in some rare cases, failure as result of burnout. The negative expressions above have the power to bruise the ego and to set our creativity, the magnificent genius of a creation we are, into a cascading motion for the better, or worse.

But if failure due to burnout ever does happen, it can't be for lack of trying. In fact, trying to succeed until exhaustion is highly commended in some cultures. An individual who has burned out trying to reach his goal will find one way or another, a different way to achieve the same goal. No matter how many times they fail, be it the second time, the third time, or the nth time around, provided he doesn't give up trying, he will achieve his goals.

Success and eventual victory are the result of refusing to accept defeat even when physically defeated. Like my grandmother used to say to me, it is all in our head; this literally means, the world, our problem, is actually the reflection of our thoughts. We would usually see and seek what we often think about, and how we choose to go about pursuing it would eventually determine our faith. Positive thinking is a key to major achievements. When it comes to our type of species, even the sky cannot begin to define our limit; only we can set and define our own limit. And no one can tell us what we can and cannot do or accomplish. Only we have that power, and the power to place value on whatever we deem is valuable and the power to make our own happiness. There is never value or happiness except for that which we bring to the table. If you want to be valuable, place some value on yourself; and if you want to be happy, do something that makes you and everyone around you happy.

This is who we are as a human species; we are an ingenuously created, emotional and responsive creatures who cannot be stopped, controlled or limited. But no one ever said being human, who we are, is going to be easy. Life is hard anyway, whatever way one chooses to look at it, whether one chooses to work or not. Life alone is work, and a work in progress that is not always fun. The act of living alone is not for the faint of heart or the squeamish. In fact, self-refining, redefining and improving anything worthy of something is hard, as it requires our attention, our skills, our commitment and our perseverance, all of which are not so easy to apply. Death, on the other hand, is easy; where the dead drops, there he stays. Unless a loved one or someone picks up the corpse, dresses it and buries it, it won't even know what happens to it. Life is precious as it is a God-given gift that should be cherished and protected.

Do not forget either the tremendous number of pressures, works and disciplines that come with life, none of which is a walk in the park, but we do it anyway. We do it because of the reward it brings us at the end of the day. We also do it because the bigger picture is not just about us and our generation, but that which is to come, and our legacy. Because of this, we are in more ways than others our own critic, our own competition and in some strange way also our own worst enemy. If we are our own enemy and we put ourselves through difficult and strenuous situations for various reasons every day, are we then any different from an outside enemy looking in and trying to harm us? Yes, we are, but only to a marginal degree. This is because we are aware of our own good and well-being, and they are not. How then can we deal with both sides of the issue to help us become an even better version of ourselves tomorrow than we are today? How can we become the very best we are destined to become, regardless of whatever loose variables may come our way?

As humanity we are all too familiar with the concept of self-sacrifice, unselfishness, humility or the ability to place others, and their needs before our own for the greater good. Sometime, we do this almost instinctively, because our hearts tell us so; it is the right thing to do. Luis didn't think twice before stopping the goal-bound ball at the goal line; he did it impulsively. In doing, he deliberately sacrificed himself so his team could win. I didn't try to pay my colleague, who tried to ruin my life, and my department manager for all the wrongs they did to me; no, I forgive and move on. I also didn't hate my biological parents for nearly cutting my life short before it even had a chance to begin; I likewise forgive and live. As humankind, we often act selflessly because we know deep down in our hearts; it is good. It is furthermore in our best interest; because humility could open impossible doors. It is liberating; as it can also frees us from the shackles the opposite sentiment could have on us. And we need to do more of it.

Overcoming anything is in a broader sense a transformational journey on its own. This is because we are often impacted by the trials in our lives, some with lasting effects. Some have discovered, and I believe this to be truth for everyone, they have become a better version of themselves at the end of a difficult and life-changing experience. And even if this story of mine has not entirely opened up your mind and helped you see things in a different light, the truth of the matter is that there are invisible forces all around us. And they are continuously affecting our consciousness as well as our sub-consciousness, the same way they are fighting for and against us.

This advice could open your eyes to an unseen world, where the impossible is possible and where the surreal, the supernatural and the things of dreams are alive and well. In fact, those invisible forces are not dreams at all, but realities that are happening to us all, but which only very few people can see. They are both forces of good and evil, and they already live among us. They are so nicely blended in; only a very special few people can tell them apart, apart from themselves. And we couldn't possibly wish them away, even if we try.

The battles that are being unremittingly waged over us and against us, the ones which are being fought around us, are the battles of good versus evil, the battles of right versus wrong and that of life and death. They are being fought over our very souls. It is real. It is a concerning and palpable issue, one for which we all should care. Don't you ever let anyone fool you and tell you something else, or lie to you that those battles do not exist, because they do. I have borne witness to that.

But in the end, the beauty of it all is that, as individuals and as a group, we ultimately have the final say in the outcome of those battles. We have the power to decide our own destiny by the choices we make. As humans, we are freely given, from the very beginning of time, the voice to choose, assuming we will wise up and make the right decision and choose life over death, truth over lies, right over wrong and good in the face of evil. Either way, we are free to choose. However, whatever decision we make would have a lasting consequence on us and our immediate surroundings. This is just how things work, for there is never an action without a reaction.

The end result of our lifelong works of building, destroying, refining, redefining and improving everything from our dreams, life, family, job, ideas, material things and more would not mean anything to us after our death. This is to say, just because we have a choice doesn't mean we can't be smart, total, and comprehensive about how we use it. Freedoms we actually have are indeed privileges that shouldn't be abused.

Gold is refined in fire for purification, so it can shine brighter. We as a species shine the brightest when we touch each other's lives in a positive way. We are better when we help others; by doing so, we are accepting ourselves, for this is who we were created to be in the first place, and in the very beginning of time. We are humane. We are by no mean a product of an accident. Being human is our identity; it is what makes us human beings. It is ingrained in our genetic makeup, our very DNA. When we are kind, generous and willing to extend a helping hand to others, we radiate unparalleled brightness throughout our own life that is far brighter than that of all combined precious metals and stones in the world. Kindness is a very powerful thing that brings joy and happiness to both parties, to the giver as it does the receiver.

Any good work must always start from the inside out. That is not to say a good work cannot also start the other way around—the outside in. But since we are on the subject of an enemy that mostly resides inside of us, meaning ourselves, it is only appropriate we start from the inside and work our way out. A pure and changed heart is far more precious than any precious stone; it is the beginning of something new, refreshing and wonderful. It symbolizes a new beginning, and in some cases a new life. Whatever work is deemed needed—whether it is changing our heart from evil to good or helping to build someone's life with words or deeds—starting from the inside is definitely a sure way to go. This is also a difficult process and should not be taken lightly. This is because not only a change of any kind is hard, people generally don't like changes. But since the enemy residing inside of us, in our heart in the form of grudges and bitterness, in our minds in the form of dirty and poisonous thoughts and hatred, is only slowly destroying us because it was never set out to help us in the first place, a change in this case and of this type is mandatory. The enemy mustn't be given room to grow if we plan on winning over it the right way. It first must to be purged at all costs. Nurturing, cherishing or coddling it in whatever form it may appear, whether it is a feeling of resentment, hate, violence or any type of non-constructive and negative feeling, is never a good idea. However, this is exactly what some of us do, and then we wonder why our transformation is not bearing expected fruits, why it is not successful. In that case, we then need to be very careful about the way we approach any radical transformation. Not doing so, could certainly result in setbacks.

Carelessness and procrastination are the two main habits for which one must look out for, as they are equally dangerous, yet easily admissible into our everyday lives. Together, they are comparable to an infiltrator, a secret spy whose job it is to sabotage people's hard work and progress. If you ever catch yourself off-guard with them, the least you can do is fight back and get rid of them, the enemy within. The same is true for corruption, and anything or anyone that is not synonymous to helping us get ahead in life. I call this letting go of the dead weights.

People who only drag you down, and never attempt to help you, motivate you and bring the best out of you, are dead weights. Hanging on to them will eventually bring you down along with them. Do yourself and them a favor and cut them loose. Contrary to what they might want to have you believe, they are not your friends. While they may in some cases be actual relatives, they don't have your best interests in mind. If they insist they do, you are simply not on their priority list. For that reason, act soon and cut them off before it is too late, before they abase you to their pit. This is because a friend doesn't hurt a friend, and any family member that is pulling its own member down isn't a true member of a family.

Put a distance between the two of you. It is often some of the closest people to us, friends, family members, coworkers, loved ones, siblings and sometimes our very own parents who represent the source of our grievances, depressions, downfalls and regressions. If this happens, we should take a moment, separate ourselves from them and think. The separation shouldn't always be physical; it could also be emotional, or spiritual. And, it doesn't have to be perpetual. It could be temporary or conditional since there is no exact science to dealing with people. With that in mind, a much-needed time to heal, to regroup, to process information and to figure out the next step is an order. But because we as a people are a complex, physical, emotional, psychological and social being, what works for one individual doesn't always work for the next person. The reason for the separation is simply because our loved ones should never be the cause of our regression in life, period. The contrary is true. They should be helping us reach our full potential.

We are not whatever anyone might have led us believe, when they said, "You are not good enough, strong enough or smart enough to do anything." Just like we have the choice between wrong and right, we also have the choice of who or what to believe, or not to believe. Again, we need to use our options wisely, by first empowering ourselves and to take a stand. A simple and innocent choice like saying, "Today I will not allow any garbage and destructive words to come out of me; the same way, I will not allow similar words to be spoken over me," could be a very powerful thing.

Overcoming from within also means being completely accepting of your full self without reservation. You must accept your qualities as well as your flaws. You must own up to your mistakes—not to revel in them, but to learn from them and move on with the self-set expectation to never repeat them. You must also be willing to work on your flaws while not letting yourself be blindsided by your qualities and recent success. As if that is not enough, you must be your very own worst critic and your very best cheerleader at once, and then find someone who would wholesomely and wholeheartedly believe in you, and cheer you to success.

If you don't start believing in yourself, it will be hard for you to find someone to believe in you. So believing in yourself and finding someone to even remotely believe in you, even by mistake, is very empowering. I once had one of my elementary teachers change the way I used to look at myself, and my life, when he sincerely congratulated me on a homework assignment. He made me believe I could do it, and that there was a genius somewhere in me. This was many years ago when I was still a young child, but I held onto it.

That teacher sincerely made me realize I had a potential. From that day forward, unbeknown to him, I made a decision. I promised myself to never let him down. I studied my hardest, did my work and turned in my assignments on time just to see the smile on his face, not just my own. That teacher had become my cheerleader, and I wanted him to be proud of me every day and every time, and he didn't even know it.

And then it hit me: This is what God is for us all along. He is our very own cheerleader who believes in us and our potential, and he never stops cheering us on to greatness and to victories, while hoping that we will notice him, and turn away from our wicked ways and come to him. To truly overcome from within is to recognize that we are never complete without God's presence in our life, and that turning to him and laying our life and burdens at his feet is indisputably the smartest thing we can possibly do in the face of life's many uncertainties.

Printed in the United States
By Bookmasters